D0334881

WHS

DRESS FOR HEALTH

Dress for health

The new clothes-consciousness

MAGGIE ROLLO NUSSDORF
AND STEPHEN B. NUSSDORF

STACKPOLE BOOKS

Dress for health
Copyright © 1980 by
Maggie Rollo Nussdorf
Stephen B. Nussdorf

Published by
STACKPOLE BOOKS
Cameron and Kelker Streets
P.O. Box 1831
Harrisburg, Pa. 17105

Published simultaneously in Don Mills, Ontario, Canada
by Thomas Nelson & Sons, Ltd.

Photographs by Mats Nordström
Fashion Illustrations by Curt Wagner
Children's Drawings by Pauletta Brooks

All rights reserved, including the right to reproduce this book or portions thereof in any form or
by any means, electronic or mechanical, including photocopying, recording, or by any
information storage and retrieval system, without permission in writing from the publisher. All
inquiries should be addressed to Stackpole Books, Cameron and Kelker Streets, P.O. Box
1831, Harrisburg, Pennsylvania 17105.

Library of Congress Cataloging in Publication Data

Nussdorf, Maggie Rollo, 1949-
  Dress for health.

  Bibliography: p.
  Includes index.
  1. Clothing and dress—Hygienic aspects.
2. Clothing and dress. I. Nussdorf, Stephen B.,
1948- joint author. II. Title.
RA779.N87 1980 613'.482 79-24029
ISBN 0-8117-0524-2

Printed in the U.S.A.

To Joseph Roschko:
A caring, generous, and wonderful friend

Contents

Foreword by Henry Haggerty   9

Preface   12

1   Learning from History   17

2   Caution: Wearing Clothes May Be Hazardous to Your Health   34

3   Synthetics   47

4   The Natural Highs   58

5   The Body Is Not Just a Hanger for Clothes   78

6   Feet and Our Bodies' Foundation   89

7   A Holistic View of Health and Dressing   97

Part 1

Part 2

8   The Natural Dresser   109

9   Texture   116

10   Color   121

11   The Basics for the Wardrobe   129

12   Little Dressing   139

13   Designs for Living   159

Part 3

14   Labels   179

15   The First Steps   186

16   The Whole Story   206

Resources for the Natural Dresser   211

Selected Bibliography   216

Index   218

Foreword

Within the last decade or so, a curiously positive social trend has evolved. Certainly we see enough evidence of discouraging trends — rise in crime, inflation, more divorces, and so on. But the relationship of buyers and sellers, users and producers, has changed in recent years, thus spawning a new and growing phenomenon — consumerism. It's an "ism" with which we are all naturally familiar, since we are all consumers, individually and collectively.

Food, clothing, and shelter are taken to comprise human beings' basic material needs. Of these, clothing has received by far the least attention in consumer terms. Although it would be trivial to say that we all wear clothes, a moment of reflection might bring to mind just how important clothes are.

First, clothing is a means of protection from the elements. Clothes are an indication of social mores as well as testimony for and against such expectations. They form a measure, however crude, by which one person perceives another.

Clothing, as any industrial product, affects and is affected by energy, environmental, and resource issues. There are energy costs associated with all clothing products. These costs differ for various clothing types, not only in the production of the fiber, the fabric, and the finished product, but also over the lifetime of the article in maintenance (such as: washing, drying, ironing) and, ultimately, in disposal. Environmental issues arise to the extent that clothing production entails industrial processes which have an impact on the physical environment. Maintenance and disposal practices also affect the environment. In the future, clothing consumption may reflect resource allocation policies, particularly in terms of natural versus synthetic fibers.

Clothes also have physical effects on people. Certain fibers may literally rub one the wrong way, contributing to skin problems. As in foods, chemicals used as processing agents or dyes can have detrimental consequences not always immediately evident. Clothing design can impede natural, physical processes unhealthily.

It is becoming commonplace that "you can't do anything anymore. Everything is bad for you somehow." There is a lot of truth in that view. Statistically, every human action carries with it some risk. Riding in a DC-10 airplane, living near a nuclear (or coal or hydro) power plant, taking a bath, wearing clothes — all are risky to various, and usually miniscule, degrees. However, by becoming more knowledgeable about what we use, we can act to minimize these risks. In seeking such knowledge, though, we must take care to look at effects that may occur thirty years in the future or three thousand miles away.

In *Dress For Health* Maggie and Stephen Nussdorf have taken the first positive step in addressing these questions in depth and providing the consuming public with information by which to make the best choices. They have treated each facet of clothing consumption thoroughly, while recognizing that the spheres of energy, fashion, economics, sensuality, health, resources, and physiology all intersect. This holistic approach makes clear the fact that consumer decisions are not made on the basis of only one or two factors. Many variables enter into a consumer's choice of clothing. *Dress For Health* will help consumers to consider all the relevant information in their clothing selection.

This is not an everything-you-wear-is-bad-for-you book. This is not a fashion book. The Nussdorfs will not instruct on how to impress friends and employers, not do they advocate a return to fig leaves and animal skins. This is a book which takes note of the relative advantages and disadvantages of clothing and design, and provides consumers with the information by which they can best satisfy their needs — now and in the future.

HENRY HAGGERTY

Scientists Institute for Public Information

Preface

Why do we wear clothes? We seem to be provided by nature with an excellent mechanism for survival — our bodies with their own skin and hair coverings. Yet, because we live in a universe whose complexity will always intrigue the seekers, perplex the solvers, and delight the rest of us, we have needs that go beyond our bodies' abilities, and we need to help our bodies interact with the environment.

Although it seems rather mundane and utilitarian, the principal reason for wearing clothes is for protection. Clothes protect our bodies from heat as well as from cold. Primitive peoples wore clothes to protect them from animals, and modern dwellers need clothing as protection in dangerous occupations, sports, and daily city living. Clothes also offer psychological and spiritual protection; the ancients wore clothing for magic and to appease the gods and evil spirits.

Clothes may protect us from feeling unloved. They can provide a womblike environment as we wrap ourselves in soft cloth and snuggle into blankets, capes, or shawls. Many children have strong attachments to articles of baby clothes, receiving blankets, or raggedy old pajama shirts. These things offer them solace when they are separated from their mothers or protection from the "monsters" in the dark. One of the first experiences a newborn infant has is a contact with cloth. In our society, a baby is wrapped in cloth immediately after birth — before it is given to its mother for feeding and cuddling. The cloth, blankets, diapers, and undershirts intervene between the baby's and mother's skins. Strong attitudes and impressions about clothing and sensuality are developed in these early stages. The cloth becomes the intermediary between the child and those who love it.

Finally, clothes offer us "moral" protection. Whether modesty is imposed by religious laws or societal traditions, clothing can keep our nakedness from prying eyes, keep us upright and distant from sensuous interactions with others, and on the whole, socialize us by creating an environment that will be uninvaded by others because of the protective barriers of zippers, snaps, buttons, and fabrics designed to conceal, cover, and prevent contact with another's skin. Only the surfaces of clothes can touch. This is desirable in protecting morals since clothes cannot feel, only bodies and skin can.

In choosing clothes, many decisions must be made. These choices are determined by our personalities, but even more so by the prevailing fashions and designs, either by an acceptance or rejection of them. However, wearing clothes is an essential part of our health and should not be subjected to whimsical, changeable decisions. We should dress for our lives, not in spite of them.

The idea for dressing for health was born on Thanksgiving and thrust out to the world to be gracefully received by our editor, Andrea Chesman, who had the courage, insight, and faith to support and nurture it into this book. We are indebted to her.

Many wonderful people devoted their skills, time, and energy to *Dress For Health*, and we appreciate the efforts of our beautiful models: Patricia Lawrence Blackwell, Drew Dixon, Carol Dysinger, Barbara Lombardo, Christopher Mathewson, Suzanne Metcalf, and Joan Roschko.

Our talented photographer Mats Nordström and gifted illustrators Pauletta Brooks and Curt Wagner lent their creative eyes and hands to help us visualize healthy dressing concepts, worked feverishly, but so patiently, under tight deadlines, and succeeded brilliantly in conveying our ideas.

We thank Amanda and Gary Carmado of Three Wishes, Dan Storper of Putumayo, Larry Rothschild and Tamara Melcher of Tamala Design with Bagel and Patsy and Reg Campkin of Little Bits for their generosity in providing the clothes and locales for the photographs and children's sketches.

To Diane von Furstenberg, Dr. Rudolph Ballentine, Wataru Ohashi, and Henry Haggerty, we offer our sincere appreciation for their gift of time and ideas about healthy dressing.

A special thanks to Goldie Shapiro, who listened carefully and helped to put our thoughts in perspective. We also thank Carol Cohagen and Egon Dumler for their expert advice.

And to our friend Helen Braun who modeled, typed, cooked, and compiled, as well as offered great amounts of support and love, we are forever grateful.

Part 1

1

Learning from history

Fashion: . . . *tastes shared by a large number of people for a short space of time.*

Quentin Bell

A Brief History of Clothes

It has been said that those who refuse to learn from history are doomed to repeat it. In the matter of dressing, this could be a mixed blessing. During certain periods, humans dressed for the right reasons: comfort and protection. But because people are subject to a variety of experiences and are influenced by what they see and hear, as well as by how they feel, dressing developed meanings beyond comfort and protection. These meanings ranged from defining moral codes to expressing social status.

Humans started to wear clothing in the last glacial stages of the Pleistocene era over 250 centuries ago. Because the climate turned so cold, these Stone Age people fashioned garments cut from furs and skins and held them together with animal tusks and bones. Their primitive clothes followed the lines of the body and protected the extremities as well as the torso and head. Since most of the body's heat is lost through the head, in extremely cold climates a snugly fitting hood was their most important article of clothing, followed by body coverings, which were folded around each other and tucked into hand and feet covers to keep the icy air out. Some natives in cold climates have adapted biologically to their environments. Their bodies have been physically conditioned over generations to withstand the rigors of the climate. They also use the natural resources such as hides and plant fibers to support their own physical adaptations. Left to its own devices, the body can adapt to its surroundings either biologically or with the help of its surroundings.

Most natives developed some kinds of leggings to protect the bottom halves of their bodies and allow freedom of movement. The upper torso was covered with capes, shirts, and dresslike garments that flowed along the body. In warmer climates, these clothes were even looser in design, and drapery developed as a good method of providing protection plus natural air conditioning — with the added benefit of style. Geometric shapes of cloth were wound around the body and tucked in at the waist or over the shoulder. Some of these draped clothes consisted of one piece of cloth that covered the body with clever wrappings from the feet to the top of the head. Others used more than one cloth, some of different shapes, to provide not only drapery but layering for warmth as well as design.

The people who inhabited temperate areas were able to drape their bodies on warm days and tailor clothes closer to the body for cooler ones. As people migrated from one area to the next, they brought their dressing ideas and customs with them. Drapery was interpreted in the Far East in the form of a kimono and in the Middle East as the caftan. Closer-fitting garments much like today's pajamas were developed in China, while the sari and dhoti (loincloth) were worn in India.

Although the people of each area appear to have developed their own sense of style that incorporated the aspects of drapery and tailoring in varying proportions, almost all cultures shared the same elemental designs — mantles, cloaks, capes, and coats for the upper body and shawls, skirts, and leggings (these in varying lengths and widths) for the lower body. It is as though the collective unconscious of design branded the minds of all developing people with similar clothing ideas that provided for their well-being. This coupled with the intermingling of cultures caused by wars, trade, and intermarriage brought an interchange of different ideas and a reinforcement of similar ones.

The use of woven textiles has been traced back over 5,000 years. Each geographical area used its own fiber: silk in the Far East; wool in Mesopotamia; cotton in India, Africa, and the Americas; and linen in Egypt.

The Egyptian linen was of a very fine quality and was almost transparent. There were few differences between male and female clothes except that women's garments were a bit longer than men's. The clothes were loose and flowing and were usually suspended from the shoulders or wrapped around the pelvis, the body's natural architectural supports. Shoes were usually sandals made from either bullrushes or leather with straps around the instep. At first the clothes were white, but when trade with other cultures introduced the Egyptians to the richly dyed finery of the East, the styles changed a little. The blouse and layering of robes were incorporated in the wardrobe, and elaborate textiles from Babylonia were used.

Mesopotamia had perhaps the most highly civilized culture of ancient times. The people lived in luxury and enjoyed decorating themselves ceremoniously with great ornamentation and style. Wool was the favored fiber, and long, heavily embroidered robes were worn over loosely wrapped undergarments. The clothes were fastened by tucking and knotting fabric ends at the shoulder and waist.

When the Persian Empire conquered Egypt in the sixth century B.C., two new garments were introduced: trousers and a seamed coat. The Persian culture relied heavily on horses for transportation, and the trousers protected the riders from the coarse hair of the animals. Coats were sewn from pelts of fur and hides, as were loose-fitting shirts. As interest in textiles developed, these clothes were made from woven cloth. The Persian coat covered the body from the neck to the knees. Undergarments were Egyptian-style — loose and flowing.

In their warm climate, the Greeks required loose-fitting clothes for comfort. Most likely, their interest in geometry and mathematics led them to develop an architectural concept of dressing, which involved wearing unsewn geometric pieces of fabric draped across body lines, creating a flow that was unsurpassed in beauty and comfort. The differently shaped clothes could be wrapped, pinned, and sewn in many ways that provided not only cool and comfortable garments but also built in pouches for carrying documents and supplies. The outer cloak, called a himation, was either draped over both shoulders or wrapped around the body, under the left arm, and pinned over the right shoulder. The garments contributed to the aristocratic lines of the body and made the wearer appear dignified and stately.

The style of Roman clothing was eclectic. They borrowed the cloths, textiles, and ideas of the peoples they conquered. However, certain garments were ascribed to Roman citizens only. These included a tunic, which was the basic dress for both men and women, and the toga, a capelike fashion that was worn as a cloak and was removed when indoors. Roman clothes included wool covers that could be drawn up to protect the head from the elements.

In the Middle East cotton was a cultivated crop. Wool was woven to make caftans and robes in the styles still worn by desert peoples today. The shirts worn in these countries were rectangular cloths with holes cut out for the head and arms. Shepherds wore a *simlah,* a seamless, hand-spun wool robe that was about seven feet wide and was wrapped and folded in ways to make hoods and sleeves.

Tailoring was more popular than drapery in the cooler climates of northern Europe, Mongolia, and Britain. Clothes were fashioned to fit the body snugly. These garments show line and form similar to the clothes of the Mediterranean world, but they concealed and covered the body more. With the emergence of Christianity in the world came a decision to adopt more covering and tailoring in the warmer countries as well. Loose drapery exposed the contours of the body; tailored clothes could hide the natural lines and comply with modesty codes better.

By A.D. 900 clothing was being affected by commerce, and with the opening of the East by explorers, the textile industry began to grow. Silks were introduced from China by the thirteenth century, and this became the most luxurious fabric worn only by the wealthy. There was a strong influence exerted by the Church, which borrowed its style for vestments from the ancient Romans, wearing white tunics and deep-colored caftans and robes. The Crusades further brought the influence of fashion and textile-making techniques from the Middle East back to Europe, and styles again intermingled. At this point in history, warriors wore heavy armor plate to protect themselves in battle. Their underclothes were quilted, and padded velvets protected their skins from the metal. Leggings and breeches were worn to protect the legs from coarse horsehair.

Although few women wore armor, the only difference in everyday dress for men and women was in the length of the garments and in headdresses. Clothing consisted of tunic-type undergarments, knee-length for men and longer for women. These were similar to monks' robes. Other garments were worn over these tunics: the *bleut,* which was a blouse, the doublet, a short, sleeveless jacket, and breeches. The legs were covered with jersey-type hose, similar to modern leotards. A mantle called the *houppelande* was worn by both men and women in the fifteenth century. This had long, wide sleeves and a small collar. A long, heavy cloak was worn over it for warmth.

It must be remembered that these clothes were worn in Europe, which had severe winters and cool summers. Houses were simple constructions, and layers of clothes were necessary to keep people warm and dry. Health considerations were still of paramount importance. Such primitive styles, invented out of necessity, lasted until the Renaissance when the whole world of art, exploration, and trade exploded, bringing about a new interest in the ancients, the worship of an idealized form in art and literature, and a thrust forward to the future.

Our most wonderful records of fashion and style of living from the fifteenth century onward has been produced by the artists of the Renaissance. Ornate, heavily detailed portraits, as well as fabrics and costume remnants, provide a historical montage and panorama of clothing styles from the high-class fashion of the royal courts to the imitative finery of the burghers to the lowly, functional costumes of the peasants.

During this period the textile world developed full-scale loom weaving and incorporated all the natural fibers that had been used only sparingly in earlier times. Silks were imported from the Orient at first, and then worms were cultivated in Europe. Until the Armada was destroyed by the British Navy, Spain was the center of wool production. After Spain's defeat in 1588, the production of merino wool shifted to Britain. This enabled Britain to expand both production and the availability of fine wools throughout her developing empire.

Up until this point in history, dressing had been a matter of protection from the elements, and maintaining health was a major consideration. Clothes covered the body with loose, flowing lines and simple styles. Fabrics were limited to the few natural fibers that were available and woven by hand on simple looms. People lived from the land and interacted with their environment on very basic levels, making clothing from the plants they grew or from the sheep they raised. Dressing was a function of living, not the reason for it as it sometimes appears to be today in our fashion-crazed world.

Yet perhaps the first symptoms of this insanity began when the developing technology of the Renaissance, though primitive, provided people with the wherewithal to change their bodily shape by tampering with their clothes. No longer would clothes be soft and simple coverings, the source of comfort and protection they'd been for thousands of years. They were to become a major factor in differentiating class from class. Textile technology literally stripped the clothes-making processes off the peoples' backs, making them dependent on machines and created a market system that dictated what they wore and when they wore it.

In the fifteenth and sixteenth centuries, fashion decisions and changes were made by the wealthy. With the rise of the middle classes, however, decisions filtered down to the nouveau riche class, who brought a distinct attitude to clothes, a type of regional chauvinism. People dressed in the costumes of their particular country or state. During this period there were terrible religious and political wars, which were felt the hardest by the serfs and peasants, whose extreme poverty was exemplified by the rags they wore. The artists of the period chose to depict the finery of the courts of Europe rather than the indigence of the masses. Only a few artists managed to paint peasants honestly, depicting their labors and their lives. These paintings show simple clothing designs and fabrics: layered tunics over breeches. In general, their clothes followed the healthy and comfortable lines that clothes had had through earlier times.

By the seventeenth century, artists depicted more of the peasants' lives and ennobled it. Poverty was seen as a kind of holy state, and the poor who were to inherit the earth were condescendingly viewed as an ignorant and childlike flock. Fashion was not permitted to them. Fortunately, as a result, they didn't suffer from the tortures and faddish designs that graced and disgraced the courts of Europe and infected the rising burgher class with opulence and waste. Instead the peasants wore simple designs, natural, hand-loomed fabrics, and warm and protective garments, that show clothing is a need for the body — not the other way around.

It was during the Renaissance that styles of dress for men and women differentiated. The development of the corset at this time was to change the shape and health of women's bodies dramatically. Centuries earlier, the women of Crete had a style of dress that enhanced a narrow waist and emphasized the size of the bust and hips. But this could not compare to the elaborate dress of the Elizabethan era with its expensive, highly decorated and voluminous clothes. These garments were styled for a corset-narrowed waist, and they were cut low in the bosom, not so much to expose the breasts, but to show off the fineness of expensive chemises and underwear. Capes and robes were still used as outer wear, but because the garments they covered were so wide, the cloaks were very long and contrived garments.

The eighteenth century heralded in the Enlightenment, a period of great cultural and philosophical development. Yet the dress of this time was anything but enlightened. It was characterized by opulence, expense, and the whims of the expansive courts of the French kings, Louis XIV, XV, and XVI. Fashion became a way of showing status and wealth, foolishness and indulgence. Clothing changed from the heavily woven textiles and cut velvets of the Renaissance to tightly fitting, lighter garments filled out by lacy underskirts. Expensive silks were used for these clothes and for outergarments.

By the end of the eighteenth century, the world was in a terrible turmoil, which culminated with the overthrow of the monarchies that had done so much to enflame the passions of enlightened and just people. As heads rolled under the guillotine, styles took on a new freedom, a kind of look of liberty. Sheer cotton dresses, with low-cut bosoms and side-slit skirts revealed bared legs. Licentious activity was paralleled in the bizarre habit of wetting sheer clothes to make them cling to the contours of the body. This practice contributed greatly to outbreaks of disease and illness.

Thereafter, interest was evinced in classical antiquities and fashion returned to the tunic and simple columnar lines until Napoleon declared himself Emperor in the early nineteenth century, when fashion again became elaborate, opulent, and costly. By the middle of the century, fashions again called for a tightly corseted waist and billowing skirts, making a woman's figure look like an hourglass. By the last quarter of the century, a woman who appeared healthy was disdained by society; a pallid, weak look was cultivated as highly fashionable. Later in the century, a bustle was added under the skirt to emphasize the buttocks. Women were dressed up and down during the latter half of the century, a practice that continues today. Steel and whaleboned corsets were felt to be necessary to "control" the figure (in much the same way man feels he must control his environment, to harness its resources strictly for his own edification and use).

The corset, which ostensibly was invented to improve a woman's figure (the selling point for women because it would make them desirable to men), not only crushed the body and distorted the internal organs, but displaced the ribs and sometimes killed the wearer. Of course the women who wore these contraptions did not work; they could barely move and were subject to fainting spells, light-headedness, and bouts of hysteria likely brought on by the inability to breathe properly and the constriction of their circulatory systems. The resulting weakness of ladies of that time was considered both charming and admirable, things that one might feel about a cherished, costly object or pet, not what one would feel about a person. But because the corset crippled a woman, it reduced her to a manageable, unthreatening object of possession, cherished by her owner, the man who remained safe from healthy and, therefore, dangerous femaleness.

Both the excesses and the repressions of the Victorian Age heralded in the nineteenth century, and nowhere were the influences of the Imperial Court of Britain felt more than in the world of fashion. During this time skirts were voluminous, bustles were the vogue, sleeves were puffy, and the body was forced into the clothes. With Victoria's death came the opulent Edwardian Age. Skirts became tighter and eventually hobbled the legs, making walking difficult.

During this period men wore suits as they had in the nineteenth century. Women's fashion was all-important; men's was merely a backdrop. There was an emphasis on men's accessories; their hats or canes being props for their important posturings. Small things were considered elegant — the crease of a trouser's leg, the turn of a cuff — but men really didn't get much fashion play until late in the century.

The First World War both exploded the world apart and condensed it at the same time. Women left the home, precipitating the need for skirts that allowed them to walk freely. The corset became obsolete, and boyish figures were the mode. Women began to like the freedom of movement and resisted the efforts of men who wished to turn the clock back on fashion and put their women back into bustles. Sportswear became an important part of couture; skirts were shortened, and freedom became an important aspect of clothes.

But social aspects caused changes again, and hemlines plummeted with the Stock Market Crash of 1929. Sober garb was the rule for the next decade. Money was scarce, and people dressed as best they could on limited resources. But by the 1930s the Second World War convulsed the world, again bringing new freedom to women while imprisoning men in uniforms. However a whole new industry emerged with the conclusion of the war, one which catapulted technology into the realm of science fiction, and at the same time hastened environmental disasters that had been predicted by social scientists generations earlier. The petrochemical industry, which made its debut in the late 1940s, introduced new methods for textile production, as well as new man-made fibers.

Synthetic-fiber production has made a tremendous impact on the clothing industry, consumers, and the environment. In the effort to compete with the beauty of nature, humans have created a poor imitation. The technological establishment believed finding synthetic replacements for natural materials would benefit society. It certainly has benefited the industry's coffers, but this has been at the expense of the ecosystem and of our health. One argument or excuse for synthetic fibers is that it mimics rare and costly natural fibers and makes more clothing available to more people. Unfortunately, only immediate costs are weighed in this equation, not long-range ones. But where health and the environment are concerned, these variables must be included.

Since the Second World War, "freedom" has been the buzz word as far as fashion is concerned. Clothing styles have become even more liberated, particularly since the political upheavals of the 1960s. Unfortunately, the choices for men are still trapped in values that are over two hundred years old: success and power. Hopefully as healthier concepts emerge, freedom will enter the picture here as well.

Choice and freedom — two words that were not a part of the fashion picture before. We believe that using this freedom to choose clothing wisely can make wearing clothes a pleasure, one that enhances lifestyles and health.

The Socialization of Dress

Fashion is a form of ugliness so intolerable that women have to alter it every six months.

Oscar Wilde

As tribal peoples developed into societies, they were able to differentiate themselves from one another and from other tribes by their modes of dress; clothes took on value as a determinant of status and class. This development could only occur when people had overcome some of the hostilities of their environments and created shelters and stable families. Trade and commerce were also necessary to obtain the natural resources needed for creating textiles and fabrics. As styles were interchanged through wars and conquests, so too were value systems and concepts of class consciousness.

Defining peoples' social status by the clothes they wore peaked in the nouveau riche society produced by the Industrial Revolution, when clothing was designed to show the wearer was in no way engaged in productive labor. Neat and spotless garments, stainless linen shirts, and wasp-waisted dresses were the insignia of that leisure class. The crippling of women by foot-binding in Imperial China was a parallel development.

Clothing today appears to establish a person's social position as it did in the past. This is particularly true with the recent proliferation of books on how to dress: for success, for power, for money, for conspicuousness in general. The upwardly mobile, middle class is encouraged to wear a uniform characterized by a good cut, quality fabric, sober colors, and a certain conformity to an ideal image. A nonconforming dresser may be viewed as someone who is, at best, not interested in success or achievement, or, at worst, a person who is subversive to society.

Clothing as a status indicator plays a strong role in the recent phenomena of the "beautiful people" — women and men who are sublimely influenced by the dictates of fashion and who pay enormous sums of money to dress in the uniforms of the rich prescribed by fashion seers and gurus. This concept goes so far as to include a category of judgment known as the "worst dressed" list (as opposed to the "best dressed" list), and the wealthy, quasi-celebrities are relegated to this list for not conforming to the attitudes and styles of the latter.

Because of social pressures, we may not be able to determine what kinds of clothes are best for us. Consciously or unconsciously, we are all in some way playing a part in life, as Shakespeare so elegantly put it, and the ways we dress help others to recognize the things we'd like them to know about us, as well as to hide the things we prefer to leave unseen. Some of us dress because we love the roles we play; others dress because they are directed by outside pressures or internal conflicts that allow them little autonomy in the clothing they choose. Nowhere is this more obvious than in the ways clothing for men and women have become differentiated.

In the early history of civilized people both men and women dressed in similar fashion with long cloaks and tunics made from geometrical pieces of cloth, covering the body to protect against the climate and hostile environment. Style and status were shown by the fineness or coarseness of the textures and fibers, by the decorative aspects of the dress, such as embroidery and jewelry, and by the personal bearing of the wearer. Certain cultures controlled the types of fibers and fabrics that could be worn by their people, but, in general, there were few differences between the dress of men and women. Because men and women are alike in functions and habits, there seem to be few physical reasons why their clothes should bear sexual differences, aside from the desire to accent these differences between the sexes, perhaps to highlight sexuality more than anything else.

By the fifteenth century, socialization of the roles of men and women was already at the state in which men were the leaders and women subservient to them. Ideally perhaps, women were the recipients of the reverence of artists and poets; in reality, they were the chattels and property of patriarchal systems and subject to their whims and fancies, as well as their fears and repressions. Women were dressed to keep them in their place. Sexual differences, as well as the subjugation of women, began their long histories when people started to define their roles by the types of clothes they wore.

Throughout primitive history all developing cultures shared similarities in clothing styles; but the rise of individual countries changed all this, as did the development of special clothes for each sex. Cultures as well as sexes were easily differentiated from each other by their modes of dress. For example, in the late nineteenth century, the bustle was at the height of fashion. This "figure improver" was a marvel of engineering that managed to distort the wearer's body so she looked a bit like a hen. A story is told that a Turkish lady asked the wife of the British ambassador: "Are *all* the ladies in your country deformed like you?" So much for the dress codes of the advanced civilizations — deformed, indeed!

But wearing clothes that altered the body did not begin in the nineteenth century. In the fifteenth century, the abdomen was the focal point of interest: the symbol of nurturing and life. Small bags of padding were sewn under clothes to fill out the area in dress similar to the way bustles fleshed out the buttocks and crinolines flared out the hips in later years.

Women were not the only ones who wore societally sanctioned contraptions. In the sixteenth century, men wore a contrivance that was to protect their genitals in battle. This was called a codpiece, originally made of metal, but then from silks and leather. It was an extension that fit over the crotch and stuck out several inches. Sometimes it was covered in fabrics that contrasted with the rest of the outfit and was decorated with jewels, ribbons, and other ornaments. Obviously the Renaissance man was not afraid of exhibitionism. The codpiece did not hurt the wearer; it just overemphasized a part of the anatomy that has since stayed under wraps.

In the 1930s Dr. J. C. Flugel, author of *The Psychology of Clothes*, believed men would be healthier if they opted for changes in their wardrobes that included some of the nicer aspects of women's clothes, such as color, lighter weight and different fabrics, layers of clothes, and the elimination of neck constriction from collars and ties. His ideas weren't heeded at the time, but men did adopt some of them in the 1960s when their fashions changed in many ways. Although the clothes did not become particularly healthy, they became more colorful and in some ways less restrictive. Men were allowed to show some creativity in their dress without appearing overly narcissistic.

By the 1960s, fashion appeared to go full circle historically, with the emergence of unisex dressing. The idea that men and women could wear the same clothes was unsettling and threatening to some people, but others accepted it as just another fashion trend. Nowhere did this trend peak as much as it did in the wearing of dungarees and jeans. Women went in droves to menswear shops to be fitted for men's pants, which don't fit women properly. This physical fact, coupled with the economic reality of a tremendous market, prompted the development of specialized designer jeans which purport to fit women properly. They obviously fit women's bodies — just like skin — but properly might not be the correct term.

Meanwhile, there remains one basic uniform for men: the dark, vested suit with a whiter than white shirt, bound at the neck with a tie. The symbolism of this outfit evokes images of morality and high ethical standards, as well as membership in an exclusive club: maleness. These are also symbols of patriarchal control; man the developer, inventor, explorer, creator is recognized by this uniform. He may lose his clout if he dares loosen his tie. How much more might he lose if he removes it?

These are but a few of the bizarre techniques that have gone into dress over the years to distort the body to an image that humans imagine excels that of nature's. However, by the 1870s several influential and fashionable people were beginning to understand the need for developing healthier attitudes about dress, Oscar Wilde among them. He advocated that women dispense with corsets and that dresses be suspended from the shoulders, not hooked tightly around the body. Wilde believed dress reformation was more important than changes in religion. As an aesthete, he could not understand how others could believe the corset-produced, tiny waist was graceful to the body. Rather, he felt it made the shoulders and hips appear too wide.

The Rational Dress Society was founded in 1880 "to promote

the adoption of a style of dress based upon considerations of health, comfort, and beauty." Mrs. Oscar Wilde, one of the society's members, lectured against tight clothing and heavily weighted dresses. She and Oscar campaigned for "bifurcated" clothes (trousers) for women, and he felt that a return to the classical Greek style of dress, with cloaks draped over good British woolens would be a tremendous improvement, both in terms of health and aesthetics.

In polite society, trousers were called "rational garments," and perhaps the most rational of these were the invention of the suffragist Amelia Jenks Bloomer. Bloomers were Turkish-style trousers that tied around the ankle and did much to emancipate women who were beginning to venture out into a more active world, which included sports as well as politics. Bloomers freed women from voluminous skirts and petticoats and allowed them to move about with dignity.

The efforts of the Rational Dress Society were, unfortunately, short-lived. By the end of the century, the society again determined to put women back in their place, this time in the form of an S-shape. The body had to be padded as well as cinched to achieve the desired results. Women as objects were expensively trussed up in colorful garments while their men preserved the sanctity of home and culture in somber garb befitting their roles as providers and leaders.

For a while it seemed that fashion was strictly the concern of women. Perhaps men just had "more important things to do." More probably, they just weren't aware of how much attention they could garner for themselves if they paid attention to what and how well they wore clothes. This has changed, and today many men are even more concerned with their images than are women.

In many respects, unisex dressing could have been the impetus for people to begin dressing in a healthy manner. Unfortunately, it was just a passing fancy, fueled by the fashion industry, and metamorphosized now into the fashion trend of the moment.

In reality what have we done with fashion? In some respects, we have inverted the silk purse/sow's ear maxim: in harming our magnificent bodies by girding them in bones and wires, strangling them with ties and laces, stifling them in unbreathing fabrics, and exposing them unprepared to the elements, we may be making sow's ears from silk purses.

Additionally, the mental pressure brought to bear on us by what is presumed to be attractive or nice-looking may be very great. People diet inexorably, perform bizarre exercise rituals in an effort to build a body that looks well in current fashion, and, in general, distort themselves to fit a very complex fashion mold.

What has allowed these vicissitudes of culture to determine what we wear? Seasonally, designers present the latest styles and fads; monthly, the magazines make their interpretations and predictions about what it all means. We are having a "sensuous spring" one moment and a "fabulous fall" the next; we're layering or stripping; lengthening or hiking; baring or concealing — and often, amid all the confusion of what to wear, we're unsure of what we'll have to look like the very next day.

Perhaps modern western society can be so easily influenced by fashions and so fickle in changing them because we have been able to control our environment so readily. If we consider other cultures, however, such as the Eskimos or Arabs, we see a different view of fashion altogether. The Eskimos, because of the harshness of their climate, need to dress in accordance with it; so too must the Arabs. Status determined by style is not a consideration in a polar-icecap igloo or a desert tent. Warmth and comfort are the essentials for survival. Frivolity here is most expendable.

The need for western civilization to change its views on dressing is becoming obvious. We may not be faced with the extremes of environment that desert nomads and Eskimos contend with, but we are affected by our chemically treated, highly industrialized and endangered world. Dressing to contend with our environment, to make us more efficient, and, ultimately, to affect our health positively may become as important an aspect of our lives as eating a sensible diet and exercising our bodies. We can learn from the times when living was more difficult, and humans had to live harmoniously with a hostile nature by adapting to it, if they wanted to live at all. We have been smug in our ability to conquer nature, cavalier in our attitudes about how we have endangered the survival of the planet. Perhaps we should take a closer look at history and revel more in the human spirit's ability to adapt to nature rather than in our propensity to change it.

Dressing for comfort or protection might be a way of repeating a history beneficial to our health. Continuing to dress for the vagaries of fashion and taste, the way we do now, might be tolling the knell of a history we would be better off forgetting.

2

Caution: wearing clothes may be hazardous to your health

Several years ago, Buckminster Fuller referred to Earth as a spaceship. Extending this concept further, our bodies may be viewed as individual spaceships, marvelous mini-vehicles, traveling through life. Most of us take very good care of whatever we use for transportation — our cars, bikes, even our skateboards. And lately there's been a renaissance of the body — eating and exercising for health.

How we clothe the body, however, seems to be an unwanted stepchild after this rebirth. It's certainly obvious that people are concerned with how they look; the billions of dollars spent every year on clothing attest to the fact that people wear a lot of them. But people have yet to realize that covering their bodies well may contribute greatly to how they feel. Concentrating on dressing in a healthy manner may have even more beneficial health effects than good nutrition and exercise.

Since we spend most of our time dressed in something, it stands to reason that anything that comes in contact with our skin — the largest organ of the body — has an effect on it. Shouldn't the things we wear be healthy and natural? In our everyday lives we are subject to a tremendous amount of environmental toxins, and many of these are absorbed by our systems through our skins.

Fiber construction is, perhaps, the most important aspect of clothes. People are very affected by the comfort of the fabrics they wear. Natural fibers are ones which breathe and flow with the natural environment. These produce the most comfort. Synthetic fibers, on the other hand, are manufactured in a laboratory. They may mimic natural fibers in some superficial qualities; but when studied carefully, synthetics cannot possibly compare in looks, feel, texture, and beauty with fibers made from living things.

Millions of pounds of chemicals are used to produce synthetics, just as they are used as preservatives and colorings in our foods. If certain chemicals are known to be harmful to the environment, and if we know that certain chemically treated foods are downright dangerous to our internal systems, just how destructive can chemically treated fabrics be to our skins? Do chemically treated fabrics damage us? Can't wearing chemicals be just as bad as breathing them? Is wearing clothes hazardous to your health?

Chemical Additives

Thousands of chemicals have been deemed toxic to humans by the various federal agencies studying the problem. Some of these are carcinogenic (agents that cause cancer); some are mutagenic, (agents that cause mutations, abrupt changes in the composition or arrangement of genes that can be inherited); still others are teratogenic (agents that damage a fetus); and some are allergenic (agents that cause skin sensitivities, dermatitis, and eczemas). Many chemicals contain properties of all these hazards (Committee 17 1975).

There is variability in the way each individual is affected by various chemicals; certain people may be more genetically susceptible to environmental toxins than others. The Environmental Mutagenic Society has determined that some individuals are "unusually susceptible to chemical mutagens."

Unfortunately, many of these known toxins are added to things we come in contact with every day: our food, water, medicines, and our clothes.

The National Institute of Occupational Safety and Health (NIOSH), the National Cancer Institute, and the Occupational Safety and Health Administration (OSHA) have begun to set guidelines for occupational safety for employees who work with these substances. Although there continues to be much debate as to the "acceptable risk" of toxic substances (If they're so dangerous, should they be permitted at all?), some progress has been made in limiting exposure to them in the workplace. Threshold Limit Values (TLVs) are set for industrial and occupational exposure restrictions; Median Lethal Doses (LDs) are set for ingestion of toxic substances; and the 1938 Delaney Amendment sets guidelines for carcinogenic additives to our foods. Yet there are no guidelines set for hazardous, toxic, carcinogenic, mutagenic, or allergenic chemicals that come in contact with our skins (and which may be absorbed through skin) daily through our wearing apparel.

The American Standards Association has designated Acceptable Concentrations Standards, which are designed to prevent any changes to body chemistry or undesirable reactions or irritations to people caused by the physical environment of their workplace. Yet there are no set standards or guidelines to determine safe limits of chemicals that are absorbed by our bodies through clothing. The Environmental Mutagen Society claims that "the guiding principle in all cases should be that no risk whatsoever is acceptable when the mutagenic compound presents no clear benefits; or when an alternative non-mutagenic compound is available." And " . . . when a useful compound already in distribution is discovered to be mutagenic, vigorous efforts should be initiated to replace it with a less hazardous compound" (Ibid., p. 509). Chemicals used in clothes should be scrutinized closely to ensure they meet with these criteria.

The Effect of Chemicals

Chemical substances may be absorbed by the body in several

ways: through inhalation, ingestion, and skin absorption. The chemical properties of the toxicant, or dangerous substance, determines which route of exposure causes the specific toxic effect. Some compounds are more toxic when they are absorbed by the skin. It seems that these are compounds that are rapidly detoxified by the liver, remaining there for a long period of time. This was determined recently by the development of rare liver cancers, called hepatic angiosarcomas, in vinyl chloride workers who developed the disease about twenty to thirty years after they'd been exposed to the substance. The vinyl chloride was not only inhaled; it permeated the skin membranes, eventually causing angiosarcomas, as well as other conditions such as anemia, dermatitis, conjunctivitis, respiratory irritations, and abnormal burning and prickling sensations of the skin.

Vinyl chloride is the monomer, or simple molecule, used in the production of polyvinyl chloride, which has a wide range of uses in the textile industry as a coating for silk and other fibers, and in raincoats and synthetic leathers. Vinyl chloride is also used in the making of elastic fibers for athletic supporters and in baby pants.

When chemically impregnated fabrics come in contact with skin the chemicals may be absorbed. The susceptibility (sensitization potential) to these substances is greatest with intimate apparel because these are in direct contact with the delicate tissue of the breasts, genitals, and other soft skin (Morrow et al. 1976). In one of the many studies done on vinyl chloride, it was discovered that the vinyl chloride monomer could migrate from one substance to another. (The monomer was proved to migrate from plastic food coverings into the food [NIOSH Toxicological Studies, 1976–77].)

The human scrotum is about twenty times more permeable by chemicals than other skin (Blum et al. 1975). To our knowledge, no studies have been done on the possibility that the vinyl chloride monomer can penetrate human scrotal tissue from athletic supporters or from baby pants. However, we feel there is enough evidence of vinyl chloride monomer migration in similar situations to warrant a closer look at the possibility.

Chemicals in clothing can also cause allergies and skin hypersensitivity, which are very difficult toxic manifestations to deal with.

It is estimated that from 10 to 30 percent of the population is affected by allergens. An allergen is a substance that causes an allergic reaction. Allergies are generally not fatal, but they can be very disabling. Usually people are allergic to a specific allergen; but if allergy-prone, they may become cross-sensitized, and, having become allergic to one chemical, may subsequently develop an allergy to a related compound. An allergic reaction is quantitative, and very minute quantities of an allergen may precipitate a reaction. Generally, the amount of a substance required to cause a response is much less than that needed to cause a systemic toxic response.

Often people are not aware of what they're allergic to. Since many of the additives to clothing are allergens, we believe that many people who suffer from undiagnosable conditions, nonspecific dermatitis and eczemas, may be allergic to their clothing — or at least to the dyes, flame retardants, solvents, and acids that are contained in them.

The chemicals in clothing that present these health hazards are sometimes a part of the basic materials of the synthetic (as in the case of vinyl chloride) and sometimes there are additives to natural or synthetic fibers. The careful consumer must be aware of these chemicals and the potential dangers they represent.

A Short Review of Synthetic-Fiber Production

The early procedures in the man-made-fiber industry used materials similar in structure to natural fibers. The materials were dissolved in chemicals and then formed into long filament fibers. Eventually, chemists began to understand the structure of fiber molecules and were able to create fibers entirely from chemical substances.

The fibrous quality needed in this process depends on the presence of long-chain combinations of molecules, called polymers. Chemists synthesized a large molecule called a polypeptide, which is a polymer containing linkages made up of carbon, nitrogen, and hydrogen (COHN). Silk and wool have this type of structure and are, essentially, polypeptides.

After developing the chemical polypeptide, the polymers must be converted into liquid form in order to be spun. Either the polymer is dissolved in a solvent or it is melted. The liquid polymer is then forced through a spinneret, which is a nozzle with a tiny opening.

In the process called melt spinning, chips of solid polymer about the size of rice grains are dropped from a hopper into a melter where heat converts the solid into a viscous liquid. The liquid forms a melt pool that is pumped through filters to remove any impurities that would clog the spinneret and is delivered to the spinneret at a carefully controlled rate of flow. These holes are usually round, but if a filament is needed in a different shape, the hole will be different. When the molten polymer emerges from the spinneret hole, a cool air current is passed over the fiber, causing it to harden. An example of a synthetic made by this process is nylon.

If the polymer is adversely affected by heat, it cannot be melt spun; therefore it is dry spun. To convert the polymer to a liquid form, it must be dissolved in a solvent. Both polymer and solvent are forced through a spinneret into a circulating current of hot gas which evaporates the solvent from the polymer and causes it to harden. Acetate fibers are dry spun.

Like dry-spun polymers, wet-spun polymers are dissolved in solvents to a liquid form. They are then forced through a jet into a liquid bath. Viscose rayon is an example.

Most polyesters are made from petroleum. The acids and alcohols used are derived from oil, but the details of their manufacturing processes are not public information. Each manufacturer has a patented process that is kept secret from other manufacturers. The most commonly used acid in the formation of polyester is terephthalic acid, and a melt-spun process is used.

Chemical Hazards

When the fibers are ready to be manufactured as textiles, they are subjected to further chemical treatments. These include all the finishing processes, among them: mercerizing, proofing (fire, water, insect), coating, bleaching, setting, and scouring. Because these processes utilize many caustic and dangerous substances as additives, we believe that there are tremendous potential — and actual — hazards posed to the consumer who wears the final products. Virtually none of the chemical additives have been tested in any great depth. Some dyes and flame retardants have met with some testing, but, on the whole, the problem has not been sufficiently observed. Perhaps, if more people were aware of the potential hazards of toxic substances in their clothes, they would demand further investigation.

The most widely publicized chemical additives to clothing are flame retardants, most notably TRIS (2, 3-dibromopropyl) phosphate, or more commonly, TRIS-BP. Because this substance proved to be mutagenic and carcinogenic in studies done on animals, the Consumer Products Safety Commission banned its use in children's sleepwear. However, the ban was not extended to its use in sleepwear for adults, hospital gowns, industrial uniforms, wigs, and other textiles used in daily life. Because of its chemical structure, TRIS is usually added to polyester fabrics. Other chemicals, such as tetrakis (hydroxyl-methyl) phosphonium (THP) are added to natural fibers, such as cotton, to retard flammability.

According to studies conducted by the Environmental Protection Agency, TRIS-BP is mutagenic to bacteria. This mutagenic activity is retained when the chemical is used to treat fabric (Prival et al. 1977). Studies have shown that some amount of TRIS is released from the fabric and absorbed by human skin. The chemicals interact at the molecular level with enzymes in the skin and are absorbed by the body chemistry. Additionally, the chemical causes allergic reactions in people who are sensitive to it.

TRIS-BP may be absorbed from sleepwear that has been washed up to fifty times and more. Washings may reduce "surface-TRIS," but the chemical deep in the fibers continues to diffuse to the outside of the cloth and is readily absorbed by the skin. TRIS-BP poses a particular risk to males who may absorb it from their pajamas through the scrotum. In studies conducted on the mutagenicity of the substance, TRIS was found to cause sterility and testicular atrophy in animals; its metabolite (a substance produced by or taking part in metabolism) was found to cause sterility in human males" (Ibid.). In another experiment, TRIS-treated pajamas were immersed in goldfish tanks. The fish died. The reason given for this was that the substance affected enzymes in the central nervous systems of the fish. TRIS is similar in structure to other flame retardants that may cause a grave threat to human health. Studies have shown that these substances are absorbed and stored in the organs (Blum and Ames 1977).

Several environmental scientists, among them Drs. Arlene Blum, Marian Gold, and Bruce Ames, have stated their concern that textile additives must be subject to testing to determine deleterious long-term biological effects: mutagenicity, carcinogenicity, and teratogenicity. They have demonstrated through their studies that people can absorb biologically hazardous chemicals in fabrics. "This absorption and the presence of a wide variety of additives in fabrics suggests the need for fabric labeling to identify additives and toxicological testing before marketing" (Blum et al. 1978, p 1023).

The flame retardant tetrakis (hydroxy-methyl) phosphonium chloride (THPC) is used with cotton fabrics. THPC is carcinogenic; and studies have shown that when wet the treated fabrics release formaldehyde and chloride. It is theoretically possible that these substances could unite to form bis-chlomethyl ether, a very potent carcinogen. This could occur during washing the treated clothes. Additionally, THPC is considered a carcinogen by NIOSH.

In 1913 William Henry Perkin published a study defining flame-proofing requirements, stating that:

A process, to be successful, must, in the first place, not damage the feel or durability of the cloth or cause it to go damp . . . or dusty. It must not affect the colors or the design woven into the cloth or dyed or printed upon it. Nothing (such as arsenic, antimony, or lead) of poisonous nature or in any way deleterious to the skin may be used and the fire-proofing must be permanent. That is to say it must not be removed even in the case of a garment which may be washed fifty times or more. Furthermore, in order that it may have a wide application, the process must be cheap. (Blum and Ames 1977, p. 195)

Interestingly, modern textile flame retardants incorporate antimony trichloride and antimony trioxide, which are highly irritating to the skin (and are absorbed through the skin). Both of these compounds are carcinogenic.

Ammonium hydroxide, triethanolamine, synthetic urea, copper napthenate, black iron oxide, and PVC-71, all known carcinogens, are used as textile flame retardants. Additionally, several known toxic substances, such as lamp black, calcium carbonate, tricresyl phosphate, and Triton X, among others, are added.

One very hazardous additive that is used for flame retardancy, solvents, dyes in textiles, and as a major component of nylon is phenol. Contact with phenol-containing products causes dermatitis. Phenol can be absorbed through the skin. In industrial use, phenol absorption through the skin can cause death within thirty minutes of contact; if death is delayed, damage to kidneys, liver, spleen, and lungs may occur (Ibid.). If phenol is absorbed through the skin, the skin wrinkles and softens. There is no pain at first, but intense burning, followed by local anesthesia, rapidly occurs. After this, gangrene sets in.

It's interesting to note that triacetate fibers are made fire retardant and receptive to dyes by impregnating the fibers with an organic solution made with a polybrominated phenol. (A bromine is a corrosive chemical element which burns and blisters the skin on contact.) To mercerize and strengthen fabrics, tetrachlorethylene and trichlorethylene are added; both these chemicals are highly toxic and may cause dermatitis.

It is hard to justify all these chemical additives. They are expensive and require expensive technology to apply them to textiles. Ames and Blum are very concerned with the toxicological problems of organic bromines, chlorines, phosphorous, nitrogen, boron, and antimony used in flame retardants today. In their words ". . . Flame retardant treatments require compromises in economy, esthetics, and wear properties," as well as present toxicological hazards (Ibid.).

Additionally, many of these flame retardants are polybrominated and polychlorinated biphenyls (PBBs and PCBs), which have entered and polluted the food chain as a result of poorly handled plant maintenance, accidents, and, in some cases, by deliberate and malicious dumping by chemical companies. Even if these chemicals weren't potentially hazardous to human skin, their use would have to be questioned because of their deleterious effects they've had on the environment. PBBs and PCBs may prove to be even more ubiquitous in our biosystem than DDT. Any use of these products places a further burden on our very fragile environment which is currently fighting a terrifying battle for survival: a battle which is, ultimately, ours.

The Dyeing of Textiles*

Dyeing processes for textiles utilize corrosive acids and bases. Many dyes are potentially carcinogenic, and almost all are extremely hazardous. Among the type of dyes used are azoic, basic, disperse, direct, fiber-reactive, mordant, and vat.

Azoic dyes are used for cellulose fibers, acetate, and triacetate. These dyes are highly reactive with human skin. Several years ago, workers who handled fabrics containing these compounds were afflicted with an epidemic of hyperpigmentation and contact dermatitis.

Basic dyes are used for wools and silks. These are known to cause allergic reactions. (Some of these dyes, Basic Orange #2 and Basic Violet #10, to name two, have been labeled possible carcinogens by the FDA.)

Disperse dyes are used for triacetate, nylon, polyester, and polyacrylonitrile (Dynel, Orlon, and Acrilan). There has been widespread dermatitis reported from the finished dyed product, as many people are allergic to them. Disperse Yellow #3 has caused dermatitis in wearers of hosiery colored with the substance; Disperse Blue #35 has induced photo-contact (stimulated by sunlight) der-

---

* Information on the hazards of dyes was gleaned from a paper by Dr. Catherine L. Jenkins, entitled ''Textile Dyes are Potential Hazards'' and discussions with the directors of the Center for Occupational Hazards.

matitis in women wearing bathing suits containing the dyes; and contact dermatitis occurred in men wearing trousers colored with the dye.

Direct dyes are used for cottons. They can be purchased in supermarkets and hardware stores and are known by brand names such as Rit, Tintex, and Dylon Multicolor. They are also used to dye leathers and as temporary hair colors. Direct dyes contain benzidines, which are highly carcinogenic. One of them, dichlorobenzidine, has been shown to have a very high absorption rate through human skin. It is also a very strong allergen and sensitizes the skin to other compounds. Dichlorobenzidine can cause anemia, jaundice, damage to the liver and central nervous system, degeneration of the kidneys, and death upon direct application of the substance to the skin.

The direct dyes in greatest production in the United States are Direct Dye Red #28, Direct Dye Blue #6, Direct Dye Black #38, and Direct Brown #95. These dyes are regulated by the U.S. government. However, many direct dyes imported here have been found to contain free benzidine which goes through the system (and is excreted in the urine, meaning it passes through the kidneys). The starting materials of these dyes are believed to be carcinogenic. There is evidence that the dyes themselves interact with the biology of the (human) host and revert back to the carcinogenic starting materials once in the body.

Fiber-reactive dyes form permanent bonds with textile fibers. There are separate types of these dyes used for cotton, for nylon, and for wool. They are capable of reacting not only with textile fibers but with human tissue. Allergies to the finished products are common.

Mordant dyes are used to deepen colors and set other dye colors in most fabrics. They are corrosive, metallic salts, usually chromium, copper, cobalt, aluminum, iron, and nickel. Many of these salts are potential carcinogens.

Vat dyes are used for cellulose, some wools, and acetate. Many of these dyes combine acids and lyes. When wet, they can cause ulcerative burns of the skin. Allergic responses have been reported to some vat dyes.

Drs. Flint and Cain have reported in *Emergency Treatment and Medicine* that poisoning from many varieties of dyes is most common in children. They claim that dye absorption from colored diapers may cause acute toxic symptoms in infants: including apathy, dypsnea, occasional gastrointestinal upsets, and convulsions (1970).

Unfortunately, manufacturers carry out only short-term tests for toxicology with the chemical additives to fabrics. No testing is done for the long-term effects of carcinogenicity, mutagenicity, teratogenicity, or allergy. In fact, the chemical industry has tried to block the development of standards to regulate environmental exposure to carcinogens and other toxic substances. Its very effective lobby has based its arguments on distorted and exaggerated economic-impact analyses. What they fail to consider, however, are the very real costs of cancer and other illnesses in humans.

More investigation is needed on the harmful effects of synthetic fabrics and their chemical additives. Negative information about dangerous chemical additives to textiles must not be suppressed. If dyes and finishes are harmful, we should know about it. It is a human right to know what's harmful to one's health. More important, we should know the alternatives to them.

And lastly — perhaps most importantly — we must be made aware of the environmental impact of all our activities, including the processes of our clothing production. The chemical-producing corporations tell us that chemicals make life possible and that without these technological advances, we'd be left somewhere in the Dark Ages. This poses a bleak picture to people who have grown accustomed to easy living, lots of labor-saving (and energy-guzzling) devices, as well as comforts that can only be achieved through a high expenditure of our natural resources. What the chemical industry fails to tell us are the facts about the effects of synthetic production on workers, the environment, and consumers. Often we don't know about water and land contamination from chemical wastes until its too late to do anything about it.

But producing polyesters, acrylics, nylons, acetates, and

fiberglass requires the simultaneous production of dangerous toxins which are released into our world. The textile industry argues that very little of our precious resources are used in making synthetic fibers, but the making of a product isn't the final involvement with it. We deal with its waste as well as its manufacture. We deal with its upkeep through specialized techniques that involve even more toxins, and we deal with the remains of synthetics, which are not biodegradable. They'll be around forever and will require tremendous energy and economic expenditures to deal with these problems.

The spaceship Earth is not a garbage scow. Intelligent awareness of the fruits of our man-made labors will ensure whether or not we've created monsters dooming us to a ruined planet or helpers for a healthy life in our world. As we must learn to control our habits of consumption, we must learn to control our clothes, from how they are produced, to how they are worn.

References

Blum, Arlene, and Ames, Bruce N. 1977. Flame-Retardant Additives As Possible Cancer Hazards. *Science* 195: 17–23.

Blum, Arlene; Gold, M. D.; Ames, B. N.; Kenyon, C.; Jones, F. R.; Thenot, J. 1978. Children Absorb Tris-BP Flame Retardant from Sleepwear: Urine Contains the Mutagenic Metabolite 2, 3-Dibromopropanol. *Science* 201: 1020–23.

Committee 17. 1975. Environmental Mutagenic Hazards. *Science* 187: 503–14.

Flint, T., and Cain, M. D. 1970. *Emergency Treatment and Management*. 4th. ed. Philadelphia: W. B. Sauders.

Morrow, R. W.; Hornberger, C. S.; Kligman, A. M.; and Mailback, H. I. 1976. Tris (2, 3-Dibromopropyl) Phosphate: Human Contact Sensitization. *American Industrial Hygiene Association Journal:* 192–97.

Prival, M. J.; McCoy, E. C.; Ames, B. N.; Gutter, G.; and Rosenkranz, H. S. 1977. Tris (2, 3-Dibromopropyl) Phosphate: Mutagenicity of a Widely Used Flame Retardant. *Science:* 76–78.

3
Synthetics

The petrochemical industry has expanded dramatically since the Second World War, not only in synthetic-production technology, but in the actual production of synthetic fibers. As with most high-technology industries, the thinking and money that goes into production far exceeds that which goes into solving the problems of waste storage and pollution. Money is spent on methods to increase profits, not on those to decrease hazards. Unfortunately, ignoring hazards will eventually lead to the elimination of any profits. Not even technology can work in a dead world.

Yet, the petrochemically produced synthetic fiber and textile industry continues to expand; in the 1970s, the total amount of consumption of man-made fibers (mainly polyesters) rose to 79 percent more than the total consumption of cotton. Milling of synthetic fibers is rising at a rate of about 8.7 percent a year, while that of natural fibers is shrinking at a slower, but steady, rate.

In the last chapter, we discussed ways that chemicals are added to clothing, particularly man-made fabrics, and how these chemicals are absorbed through the skin. Synthetics, however, are of special concern to health-conscious dressers, not only from the point of view of their chemical make-up, but also from the point of view of comfort. Many synthetics are highly unabsorbent and become extremely uncomfortable in warm weather. Others are produced at great cost to our environment. This chapter examines various synthetic fabrics by generic name and describes the health aspects and environmental costs of each.

Natural fibers come from either protein (animal) or cellulose (plant) sources. Synthetic fibers are produced from minerals which are subjected to chemical synthesis to produce fiberlike characteristics that mimic the forms of natural fibers. The first commercial uses of man-made fibers began forty years ago with the advent of nylon in 1939. Until then, clothing was made from natural fibers: cotton, silk, linen, and wool.

There are over seventeen generic names to these chemically constructed fibers; they include nylon, polyester, acrylic, and modacrylic, among others. These are the fibers that we encounter the most in clothing and the ones about which the health-conscious consumer should have an awareness.

Nylon

The name nylon has no real meaning. When the fiber was invented by E.I. du Pont de Nemours and Co. in the 1930s, the name was thought to be easy to pronounce, short, and catchy. For years, man had been trying to discover a fiber that could imitate the marvelous filament creation of the silkworm. The discovery actually was accidental. After repeated unsuccessful experiments with chemical compounds, the laboratory workers decided it was impossible to create what they wanted. One of them filled a hypodermic needle with some of the warm solution they had been working with and sprayed it into the air. The stream of liquid cooled on contact with the air and formed a filament. After more experimentation, this filament was found to have qualities that could be used for fabrics. This original fiber was called nylon 6,6, which described its chemical composition. It was presented to the public at the 1939 World's

Fair. Soon other countries developed their own formulas for producing the fiber.

During the war years silk was prohibitively expensive. Much of the silk produced was used for parachutes. The novelty and durability of the new fiber won the hearts of many women. It was a symbol of true love to be given a pair of nylons.

Because nylon was a replacement for silk, the jaws of silkworms were studied in order to create a spinneret similar to the worms'. A perforated plate with tiny holes through which the liquid chemicals could be forced into a stream of air was developed. The warm liquid cools on contact with air to form a filament which is then spun onto a bobbin.

The raw materials used in nylon formation include coal, petroleum, natural gas, and water. When petroleum and natural gas were viewed as cheap and expendable resources, as they were in the 1930s, the manufacture of nylon was considered a boon to the economy and the textile industry alike. However, we are all now aware that these resources are limited and unrenewable. They are also becoming expensive. In fact, the production of nylon could make clothing made with it even more expensive than silk in the long run.

Nylon fabrics are not porous and do not allow air to circulate, particularly if the fabric is tightly woven. They do not conduct heat well either, and moisture can't pass through the weave. Heat may build up in both the fabric and the body, making nylon very uncomfortable in some cases. It is particularly unsuitable for wear in warm weather because it does not allow perspiration to evaporate from the body, creating an unhealthy environment on the body's surface. Nylon stockings can be very unhealthy in summer months, particularly in the crotch area where bacteria can breed in the moist environment. Some hose are made with a ventilated cotton crotch to allow for some air circulation. This type of garment is better than the original pantyhose, but these still do not allow air to circulate around the legs and, if too tight, can inhibit circulation. Nylon's low absorbency makes it feel clammy and uncomfortable in warm weather. Sports people should be aware that nylon sports gear will often make them feel very warm and prevent them from cooling their bodies properly after exertion.

The chemicals added to nylon finishes can be very harmful to skin. Formaldehyde, an allergen, is a necessary additive in making the fabrics flameproof and in setting dyes. This can be absorbed by the skin, cause dermatitis, and make the feel, smell, and general quality of the garments very unpleasant.

Polyester

Polyester's history is similar to nylon's. In an effort to mimic nature, chemists tried to create a perfect fiber; in our estimation, similar to Dr. Frankenstein's desire to create a perfect man. In the case of the polyesters, science has succeeded in creating a textile monster — a nonbiodegradable nightmare formed by the marriage of acids and alcohols.

The first polyester fabric was produced in 1951 by du Pont and was called Dacron. Since that time many different types of fibers and fabrics have been created — Kodel, Enka, Avlin, and Trevira among them. Each bears the imprint of an assembly-line look and feel, factors distasteful to natural dressers whose individuality is offended by such uniformity.

Polyesters are derived from petrochemicals. The process for creating fibers is similar to that of nylon production: the liquid chemicals are forced through a spinneret and then cooled. Unlike silk, whose filament size is determined by the jaws of the individual worm, polyester filaments can be man-controlled and manipulated. The fibers can be regulated to mimic the look, but never the actual texture and feel, of linen. The technology freely used for over two decades of polyester developments is now becoming expensive. Because these fibers are petroleum-based, the possibility of creating this type of fiber inexpensively is diminishing.

Polyesters tend to absorb oil from the skin and hold oily stains in their fibers, making them difficult to clean. They do not absorb body moisture and are extremely warm and uncomfortable in warm weather. Neither do they conduct heat well, which makes them unsuitable for winter wear. These fabrics are susceptible to melting if exposed to flame and sparks. A cigarette ash can burn holes in a polyester garment. Most of the newer polyesters are dyed with disperse and basic dyes, which are known to be allergenic and corrosive to human skin. These are also potentially carcinogenic.

Acrylics

Like nylon and polyester, acrylics were developed in the du Pont laboratories in the 1930s. They, too, are derived from petrochemicals. The first commercially successful acrylic fiber was du Pont's Orlon, which was marketed in 1950. Soon other fibers were introduced including American Cyanamid's Creslan and Dow Chemical's Zefran.

Orlon

Orlon is made from acetylene or ethylene, both petroleum derivatives. These are treated with acids, and the results are dissolved in solvents, then forced through a spinneret. The fibers cool into a filament and are then stretched. They are typed for the various uses, such as for bulky knits, blankets, or socks. These fibers can be spun into soft yarns similar to wools, but have a tendency to form little balls of yarn called pills in the surface of the fabric.

Orlon is weaker than cotton, silk, and linen; it is the weakest of the acrylic fibers. It does not stretch or give well. It also doesn't conduct heat and is, therefore, warm; but it has low absorbency and does not allow perspiration to evaporate from the body. This could make the wearers extremely uncomfortable particularly if they exert themselves while wearing Orlon garments. Manufacturers claim that Orlon sweaters are as warm as wool ones, but in reality they do not have the breathability of woolen fibers and provide only an artificial warmth and not a comforting, living, and natural one.

Acrilan

Acrilan fibers are formed by a more complicated process than that for Orlon. Gases are combined to form ammonia, which is combined with natural gas to form an acid. When natural gas is heated, it forms acetylene, which is combined with this acid to produce acrylonitrile. This is then changed into powder form, dissolved in a solvent, but instead of being put through a spinneret, it is put in a bath to coagulate the fibers. These are then dyed and stretched. Like Orlon, there are many types of Acrilan for various uses.

Acrilan is a bit stronger than Orlon, but still weaker than cotton, silk, and linen. It does not stretch well, but is highly insulative. Like Orlon it is not absorbent and does not permit perspiration evaporation, making it uncomfortable for warm weather wear.

Creslan

The method of deriving Creslan acrylic fiber is still more complicated than that for Orlon and Acrilan. Suffice it to say the gases are combined to form acrylonitrile, dissolved in solutions, and forced through spinnerets to form filaments. The filaments are washed to remove the solvents and are then stretched. They are typed for their various uses.

Creslan is a bit stronger than the other acrylics, but not as strong as natural fibers and, therefore, is not as long-wearing. This fiber is a bit more comfortable than Orlon or Acrilan for most climatic conditions. Since it blends very well with natural fibers to provide durability and to make the fabrics lightweight and comfortable, they are not as unsuitable for natural dressers. However, finding a suitable blend may be difficult and anyone sensitive to the chemical components of acrylics may find themselves allergic to this fiber.

Zefran

Dow Chemical Company, makers of Zefran, will not disclose its manufacturing processes for the fiber. The procedure is probably similar to the formation of the other acrylics. Again, these are typed according to their uses.

Zefran is the strongest acrylic fiber, but it is still weaker than cotton, linen, and silk. It is a bit more absorbent than the other acrylics and, hence, more comfortable. It is not very elastic. Zefran may be worn by natural dressers when it is blended with natural fibers to give strength and resiliency to fibers that are comfortable and healthy. Again, it's important to be aware that some individuals may be sensitive to some of the fiber's chemical properties. If discomfort to the skin's surface is felt, wearing blends should be discontinued.

Modacrylic

As the name implies, modacrylics are modified acrylic textiles. This means the acrylonitrile compound is combined with others to form new properties. Union Carbide developed Dynel, a combination of natural gas, salt, ammonia, and water in the 1950s. These ingredients form three chemicals — acrylonitrile, vinyl chloritrile, and vinyl chloride. Vinyl chloride is a highly toxic substance known to be carcinogenic in humans. When these substances are combined, they form a powder which is dissolved in a formula similar to that used in nail-polish remover. The solution produced is forced through a spinneret, cooled in a water bath, dried, and stretched. Dynel is used for fake fur coats and wigs.

Dynel is weaker than cotton, silk, and linen and is not very stretchable. It is the least absorbent of textile fibers and extremely uncomfortable in warm, humid weather. This fiber must be dyed with direct dyes, which can be absorbed by the skin. Because Dynel contains vinyl chloride, it should be carefully considered when worn close to the body, particularly in a wig worn on the highly permeable skin of the scalp. Natural dressers concerned with the vinyl chloride problem would be better off avoiding this fiber.

SEF Modacrylic

Similar in structure to acrilan, SEF Modacrylic is extremely uncomfortable in warm weather and much weaker than the natural fibers, nonbreathable, and nonporous. The fiber was developed in response to the need in the textile industry for flame-retardant fabrics. Unfortunately, this extremely unhealthful, uncomfortable fiber is used for infants' sleepwear, sweaters, and pram suits, as well as in blends for adult apparel. Tremendous concern has been shown about the possibility of some flame retardants in clothes migrating from the fabric through the skin. Many of these man-made fabrics are constructed with toxic substances. These inherently flame-retardant fibers do not require additional toxic additives, but contain harmful properties in their make-up. We think this should be a concern of natural dressers, particularly in choosing their children's wardrobes because children are particularly sensitive to chemicals. These fibers lack absorbency and do not permit perspiration evaporation. The damp environment on the skin's surface not only creates an atmosphere for discomfort, it is also a potential breeding ground for rashes. Damp skin may also allow the fiber solvent to dissolve, causing dermatological reactions.

Other Synthetic Fibers

Spandex

Spandex is a man-made fiber that gives elasticity to clothes. These fibers can be stretched up to seven times their length and then return to a relaxed state when the tension is released. Spandex is made from polyurethane linked with hard segments to strengthen it. Originally, elasticity was added to garments with rubber products. Rubber deteriorates when it is exposed to skin oils and doesn't take dyes readily.

Nylon filaments were also used to elasticize clothes, but the stretchability wasn't as good as that of rubber. Nylon is used, however, to add stretch to socks and hose.

Du Pont developed the first spandex fibers in the 1940s and began marketing it under the name Lycra in the early 1960s. Other names are now used, and many companies produce the fiber, so that spandex is now used in virtually all stretchy garments.

The manufacturing processes for spandex fibers are closely guarded secrets. The processes, however, are similar to the production of other man-made fibers: chemicals are combined, soaked in solvents, spun or forced through spinnerets. They are made receptive to dyes or whitened with other caustic agents and solvents.

Spandex fibers do not conduct heat away from the body. In fact, heat will build up in the body in areas covered by the fiber. They are not absorbent, which makes them uncomfortable for wear in warm weather. Interestingly, most swimwear made today is made with a large percentage of spandex fibers — uncomfortable fibers for uncomfortable weather. Also, dance wear and sportswear incorporate the fibers for stretchability. Spandex bodysuits are very popular garments worn today. For more comfort and healthfulness in these clothes, we recommend the fabric be blended in a ratio of 75 percent cotton to 25 percent other fibers, including spandex. Some manufacturers are aware that people need to be comfortable when they're active, and a careful consumer can find these high-cotton-blend elastic clothes in many shops and department stores.

Spandex is also used for underwear and girdles. These tight elastic fibers can seriously constrict the body's tissue leaving unsightly marks, as well as cut off circulation and prevent the skin's pores from breathing. The fibers also have a paradoxical use in support garments, such as support hose recommended by some doctors for people with varicose veins. The support provided by the stockings may make people feel less pressure in the legs while they are wearing them, but at the same time can constrict blood circulation in the legs exacerbating the vein condition. Proper nutrition and exercise are much more effective treatments for circulatory problems than wearing support clothing. However, if they are prescribed by a medical practitioner, the wearer should be careful to put the clothing on properly. They should be put on before the body has engaged in the day's activities, before gravity has a chance to exert too much pressure on the legs and abdomen. This is best done as the person gets out of bed in the morning. They should also be removed when the person has completed the day's work. At this point the person should recline with legs supported on an incline so circulation can return to the legs.

Olefins

Olefins or polypropelene fibers are related to wax. They are prepared through chemical synthesis and produce fibers that can be used in some wearing apparel. These fibers are virtually nonabsorbent and are very uncomfortable on the skin. Consumers concerned with comfort should be aware that Marvess, Olefin, and Vectra are polypropelene garments and may be unsuitably warm for clothing.

Saran

Saran is created through chemical synthesis of petroleum derivatives, chlorine, and vinyl chloride, a highly toxic carcinogen (which provides up to 8 percent of the weight of saran fibers). The fabric produced from saran is nonabsorbent. The fibers are not usually used for underwear or clothing worn close to the skin, but are used for outer wear. These fabrics do not conduct heat well and will burn from cigarette sparks. They are used for raincoats because of their inherent water repellency. Natural fibers are much more comfortable, pliable, resilient, and breathable than this fabric made from dangerous, caustic materials.

In constructing or manipulating the chemical structure of a material lots of things can be built in. Unfortunately, in the case of synthetic fabrics, comfort seems to be the one thing that's impossible to add. In fact, it appears to be built out of these fabrics.

In the fiber-comfort comparison chart that appears at the end of chapter four, it can be seen that synthetic fabrics are not as comfortable as natural ones. Absorbency is a determining factor because of the effect moisture has on the skin. A wet or clammy feel is discomforting to the body and spirit. Synthetic-fiber garments can make individuals feel ill at ease or contribute to their feeling unwell simply because they do not allow the skin to breathe.

But comfort, or the lack of it, and potential bodily hazards are not the only aspects of synthetic fibers that make their use objectionable. The impact of production of these fibers is something that consumers must become aware of in order to make a decision about demanding, purchasing, and wearing them. In determining value, one must consider costs on every level — including wasted fuel resources and environmental pollution.

Synthetic-fiber production is ecologically unsound; non-renewable fossil resources are synthesized through an elaborate process that requires the burning of more fuels and causes the release of toxins into the air and water systems to produce the substances that have an interminable lifespan and which eventually end up as nonbiodegradable garbage.

Fortunately, nature in its sagacity created natural fibers that produce beautiful, comfortable garments that have a natural lifespan. Humans are biodegradable. There's no reason for their clothes to outlive them by infinity. Synthetic fibers are not only unnecessary for the existence of life, they can prove harmful to it. Natural fibers are not only necessary, they are beneficial and comforting to life on the planet.

4

The natural highs

Fibers that are gleaned from plants and animals are called natural fibers. Clothes made from these fibers feel good against the skin. They absorb moisture and provide insulation from the elements. Natural fibers run the gamut from luxurious silks and wools to common, but comfortable, cotton — and according to the Opinion Research Corporation, a consumer's first consideration in buying clothes is comfort.

Because these fibers are formed in nature they place little stress on the environment. Modern harvesting and growing techniques place a high-yield demand in linen and cotton crops, and some of these techniques can be ecologically detrimental, but the problem lies in the technique, not the product. Carefully managed and controlled plant production can be ecologically sound. Wool and silk production do not stress the environment. The animals are bred, and the fibers are harvested from them — wool from sheep and silk from worms. All use a renewable resource, the sun, as their source of energy. They do not require secondary energy sources and intense heat for their production as do man-made fibers. They are all biodegradable, returning to the earth after their lifespan to be decomposed by bacteria and returned to the soil as nutrients for new plants and animals.

Natural fibers are easy to care for. With a little instruction and common sense, consumers can easily launder and clean garments made from animal or plant sources, and none of the fibers requires environmentally unsound processes to preserve its look and wear.

In an age when convenience, time, and labor-saving devices are considered essential, the incredible number of man-made, self-pressed, wash-and-wear fabrics appears to be a panacea. But if we really stop and consider the costs of these labor-saving consumables in terms of energy spent in producing them, as well as the sacrifice one makes in terms of feeling good to wear them, they really save us little. A dress may look terrific on a hanger, but unless it fits the body well and its fabric feels good on the skin, it's a worthless object that will probably go unworn and end up somewhere in the back of a closet.

Natural fibers are sometimes considered the fibers of the rich because many of them are very expensive. However, a careful consumer interested in health as well as value and luxury can find the best long-term investment is in finely made, naturally processed clothes that are simply and elegantly fashioned from nature's gifts—plants and animals. These gifts form the basis of the textiles that should comprise the wardrobe of the natural dresser.

Textile fabrics and yarns are comprised of fibers that are fine, hairlike substances which can be woven into cloth. Wool and linen are easily spun and were the most commonly used fibers until cotton production became automated during the Industrial Revolution and thus became more readily available. Silk, a very strong and pliable textile fabric, has been cultivated for thousands of years.

Natural fibers then, as now, provided clothing for all types of climates and weather conditions as well as very fine fabrics for high fashion and ornamentation. Textile production was on a much smaller scale than we know it today, and people were able to see the manufacture of clothes virtually from start to finish: from the planting, harvesting, and spinning of cotton, to the farming of silkworms, to the herding and shearing of sheep and the weaving of their fine wools. Textile manufacturing expanded with growing industrialization; but for centuries, people relied on the gifts and fickleness of nature for their raiment.

This started to change in the twentieth century with the development of man-made fibers. It now seemed that man needn't rely totally on nature to provide for clothing — science could provide fabrics almost just as well. The chemical components of natural fibers could be mimicked in the laboratory, and textiles could be created in a test tube.

There were, of course, advantages to these procedures. Manufacturers could control all the variables of production, insuring quantity and quality control. Boll weevils do not attack steel vats of triacetate. In an industry as large as textile manufacturing was becoming, control and efficiency of the modes of production was becoming more important. The fact that looks, feel, and comfort may have to be sacrificed to achieve optimum output matters little on the bottom line of annual reports to stockholders. Industries thrive on efficiency, inventories, and sales — not comfort.

Like all things in nature, natural fibers are subject to subtle variations in look, texture, and feel. Cotton grown in one area may have a different quality from that grown in another; the wool of one breed of sheep may differ significantly from that of another breed. These variations are aesthetically desirable because they allow for interesting and unusual dye and texture effects, for shading and gradations of light. The whole idea of the lack of uniformity in the natural fibers presents a broad palette for both designers and dressers alike to create their own individual wardrobes. Just as no two snowflakes are alike, no two cotton or wool or linen yarns are, and as snowflakes build texturized, crystal drifts, so too do the unique woven fibers create textures that enhance the wearer.

In terms of their comfort, use, and modes of production, however, natural fibers are more alike than not. Yet, there are enough differences in the fabrics to enable a natural dresser to choose from a wide variety of seasonally varied clothes with different textures, weights, and feel — without ever resorting to synthetics. A look at the different types of natural fibers shows how adaptable these materials can be.

Cotton

Cotton is one of the oldest fibers used by humans for clothing. Historians have evidence of its use as far back as 12,000 B. C. It is believed to have been cultivated first in India and Pakistan and then to have spread further east to China. The early Egyptians wore cotton clothing as did the Phoenicians, Persians, and Hebrews. Tribal merchants introduced cotton cloth to the peoples of the Mediterranean, and both the Greek and Roman civilizations adopted the fabric for their togas before the Christian era began. Nomadic Moslems cultivated cotton for clothing in African and Asian desert areas. In the Western Hemisphere, fragments of cloth from Aztec ruins indicate the fiber was woven there over seven thousand years ago. The Incas of Peru wore cotton clothing, and native Americans cultivated cotton crops as early as A. D. 700.

Cotton spinning and weaving started to develop in Europe, and in the thirteenth and fourteenth centuries history records that Columbus took cotton yarn back to Spain from the Americas as evidence of the high level of culture he had found. The Portuguese explorer, Vasco Da Gama, reported finding cotton crops off the coast of East Africa in the late fifteenth century.

Industrial developments of the eighteenth and nineteenth centuries, such as the spinning jenny and frame, the cotton gin, and the power loom greatly expanded the production of cotton cloth. The new processes gave the cloth a soft finish. The development of durable press finishes and methods to control shrinkage have all contributed to making cotton the most widely used clothing fiber in the world.

Cotton requires a long growing season and warm temperatures. The plants, which reach a height of three to four feet, grow quickly once they sprout — about two weeks after they're sown. Blossoms appear about two months later, and the plants selfpollinate. Soon the petals drop off and leave a pod-like boll, the ovary of the plant. Within two more months the boll ripens, splits open, and exposes the soft, moist, and fluffy white fibers within.

There are several varieties of cotton, and this determines the size and number of fibers within the boll, which range from one-half to two inches in length. The finest strain of cotton grown today, which is used for cotton clothing, is a crossbreed of American Pima (the type planted by early native Americans) and Egyptian cotton.

Cotton is machine-harvested, ginned to remove the fibers from the seeds, pressed into bales, and shipped to spinning mills for additional processing. Any leafy matter is removed in the carding process, which also separates matted fibers. Some fibers are additionally treated to combing, which refines them further to be used for very fine clothing fabrics. The fibers are then spun into yarn and woven or knitted into cloth. Some common cotton fabrics are velvet, denim, canvas, poplin, muslin, corduroy, broadcloth, oxford, percale, terry, and damask.

Cotton is the most comfortable of fabrics because of its porosity and breathability. The pores permit body-moisture evaporation, and air can pass through the cloth.

Under a microscope the single, elongated cell of cotton looks like a spiraled tube with a twisted, rough surface. The twists average about 250 per inch, and finer grades of cotton have more condensed spirals. This natural twist makes cotton easy to spin into yarn; with more twists, less spinning is needed to produce a strong, soft yarn, hence a comfortable clothing fabric. In a public opinion survey, men chose cotton on an average of two to one over polyester simply because of the feel of the fabric against the skin.

Sometimes it's desirable to remove the natural twist in cotton fibers to produce a smooth, lustrous surface in the fabric. This is done by mercerizing, a process which causes twisted fibers to swell and straighten. Light reflects handsomely off mercerized cotton, and this type of fabric is useful for some types of clothes. Mercerized cotton is very strong, absorbent, mildew-resistant, and receptive to dyes.

The absorbency of cotton is an important factor for comfort in clothes. Its construction transmits perspiration and heat away from the body. Cotton fibers dry quickly; this is helpful in keeping the body dry as well. Bleached cotton reflects heat, making garments made with the fabric perfect for warm-weather wear.

Cotton is also useful for clothing worn in cooler weather. Warmth in clothes depends upon air that is trapped within the fabric. Some cottons, such as corduroy or velour, are perfectly suited for cooler weather because of their thickness. Quilted and layered cottons also make good, cool-weather clothes. Quilted garments, worn for thousands of years by the people of Asia, provide a tightly woven outer layer which protects against the wind and softer, inner layers interspersed with air. Flannels make good cotton clothes for cool weather as well. These are napped fabrics, ones on which the surface has been brushed, which provides warmth because the brushing process creates insulating air cells. Naps may be made thicker by brushing one side of the fabric in one direction and the other side the opposite way. A thicker nap provides more air cells and hence more warmth.

Another important characteristic of cotton is its washability. Cotton clothing may be hand- or machine-washable, depending on the dyes used on the cloth, and is usually machine-dryable. It can be boiled and bleached with few ill effects and is well suited for use in underwear and infants' garments. Cotton may be ironed or steamed to remove wrinkles. Dry cleaning is usually not necessary, but will not harm most cotton fabrics. Some cotton garments do not require ironing because of special manufacturing wash-and-wear treatments, but even untreated garments hang out well and may require only a touch-up to restore freshness.

There are few drawbacks to cotton clothing, but one or two are worth mentioning. Unless it is specially treated, a cotton garment may be susceptible to mildew, which is caused by a fungus that thrives on damp cloth. Mercerization helps to prevent mildew, but it's also important to keep cotton clothes dry to avoid having the rot eat away at the fabric. Cotton also shrinks. This is an important consideration in purchasing 100 percent cotton clothing. Clothes that have not been preshrunk by the manufacturer may shrink more than 3 percent in washing. A dress or shirt that shrinks a whole size in the wash is not a good buy, nor a comfortable one. In checking labels, it is wise to determine whether or not the garment has been sanforized, a process which minimizes its shrinkage, and if not, to buy a size large enough to allow for shrinkage.

Cotton fabrics resist fading from cleanings and perspiration and lend themselves to every conceivable type of clothing. Men, women, and children are all very comfortable and fashionable in clothes made with this versatile, soft fabric.

Linen

Linen, a bast (phloem) fiber that comes from the stem of the flax plant, has an incredibly long history. The Neolithic Lake Dwellers of Switzerland wore linen garments over 10,000 years ago. The Egyptians, who believed the goddess Isis created linen, were buried in shrouds made from flax, and the temple priestesses wore only white linen garments in homage to Isis. Linen was considered a regal fabric in the Middle Ages and today is thought of as a prestige fiber since it is difficult and expensive to produce. Garments woven of flax are exceedingly elegant and beautiful.

Most of all the flax grown is either in Belgium, which produces the finest linens, or in the Soviet Union, which has the most flax acreage in the world. A good moist and mild climate is essential for its growth, and the plants require more care than cotton. Flax production and harvesting have traditionally been done by hand, a laborious process involving much time and skill. This has made its production prohibitive for most countries.

Flax plants grow to a height of three feet, topped with blue or white flowers and linseed bolls. The pithy center of the stem is surrounded by the flax fibers. They require little care until harvesting when the stalks are pulled up by the roots to insure long unbroken fibers which can be spun into yarn easily. The plant is then processed with rippling, which removes the seeds; retting, or soaking, which loosens the flax fiber from the straw; scutching, which removes fibers from the woody stalks that have been dried; and hackling, or combing, which is similar to the process used for cotton.

Linen is very desirable as a clothing fabric because of its body and strength. The plant fibers come in thick and thin bundles which give a lovely array of textures to fabrics. Flax looks very similar to golden-colored straw. It is twice as strong as cotton, extremely absorbent and porous. It is a wonderful fabric for clothing worn in warm weather because of this porosity. If it is blended with cotton, its durability increases and its cost decreases. Like cotton, linen dries quickly and keeps moisture and heat away from the body. The fibers are smooth, long, and hard and do not spot or stain as readily as cotton. This surface also makes linen resistant to bacteria.

Linens often dye unevenly, which adds to the beauty of the finished product because the textures lend themselves to unique patterning. Because it has good body, linen drapes well around the body. Flax garments shrink less than cotton ones. They are not damaged by moths.

Though expensive, linens are wonderful for underwear because they are so comfortable close to the body. They are also durable enough to give years of wear and may be boiled to be used as sanitary dressing garments.

Linen garments may be washed in very hot water, over and over for years. Repeated washings enhance the fabric's softness. White clothes should be dried in the sun to preserve their whiteness. Although it's usually not necessary, linens may be dry-cleaned. They do not attract dust, so cleaning is necessary less frequently than for other fabrics.

The drawback to linen fabrics is wrinkling. Flax fiber is not elastic, and linen fabrics must be ironed frequently. Some linen garments are treated for crease resistance, but the process weakens the durability of the fabric. Linens should be ironed while damp and should not be starched too heavily because the process weakens the fibers. Linen is also susceptible to mildew and must be kept and stored dry. Because of the natural inelasticity, garments made from linen must not bind or pull at the seams because this might make an otherwise very comfortable cloth unsatisfactory at the waist, neck, or armpits.

Other plant fibers, similar to flax, have been used for centuries in clothing and related articles. Ramie, or grasscloth, is an extraordinary natural fiber that is used as a substitute for linen. It is believed to be stronger than wool or flax, more absorbent than flax, and resists mildew. Ramie garments have a smooth, lustrous appearance, keep their shape, and resist shrinking.

This little-known fiber is grown mostly in the semitropical areas of China, Egypt, Europe, and East India. It has been grown successfully in some parts of Georgia, Mississippi, Texas, and the Florida Everglades. Unfortunately, U. S. processors have not found ramie to be profitable enough. They have experienced difficulties with spinning the fibers. Obviously, no one here wants to retool to spin this fiber the way it is done in Europe (like silk). In order to get the capital to make ramie production profitable, the producers would have to put up quite a fight against strong competition.

Hemp and jute are cellulose fibers that do not lend themselves for use as woven cloths. They are, however, used for shoes, rope-type belts, and strong threads.

Silk

Silk is the fiber of great legends and beauty. Over five thousand years ago the Chinese Empress Si Ling Chi, the venerated Goddess of the Silkworm was said to have accidentally dropped a worm cocoon into a cup of hot tea, which loosened and softened the fiber until she was able to pull away a continuous strand. This discovery gave birth to the silk industry which was to be guarded with the highest security of any industry ever. In fact, revealing the secrets of silkworm cultivation was punishable by death. Other industries grew up around the worms, the most important being the cultivating of mulberry trees as special food for the valuable, talented creatures. China managed to keep her secret for almost three thousand years. But legend tells us that two monks sent from Byzantium risked their lives and managed to smuggle silkworm eggs and mulberry seeds in their walking sticks to the Emperor Justinian, who then learned sericulture and started its spread through the Mediterranean.

Moslem conquests helped spread this knowledge through southern Europe. By A. D. 900, the industry was flourishing in Spain. Soon after, Italy developed the science and by the twelfth century was the world's greatest and finest producer of beautifully woven silks, a position held until France excelled in its production nearly five hundred years later.

The Far East was not idle during these centuries of silkworm cultivation. The desire for knowledge of this elegant fiber was so great that the Japanese kidnapped four Chinese girls and forced them to reveal the secrets of sericulture. By A. D. 300 Japan had its own industry started. Intermarriage among monarchs has done much to spread religions, politics, languages, and philosophies to other lands. The union of a Chinese princess and an Indian prince spread silk cultivation still further in the world.

England started sericulture in the sixteenth century, but the climate was not conducive to the healthy growth of worms. The industry was introduced to the American colonies in the eighteenth century, and several colonial areas were granted money to grow and cultivate both mulberry trees and worms. However, silk cultivation is extremely costly, and although much of the world's silk is today woven on American looms, the actual silk is usually imported from Japan and Europe.

The cultivation of *Bombyx mori,* or silkworms, requires great care to produce the durable fibers that end up as beautiful fabrics. Silkworms pass through four stages in their short lives and in each stage must be kept in quiet, sanitary beds of straw. The life cycle starts with eggs that hatch into caterpillars, which then spin the cocoons for protection to permit its development into a chrysalis. This emerges as a moth, which lays eggs to start the cycle over.

The silkworm takes three days to spin its cocoon, composed of a protein substance and sericin, a gummy substance that cements the cocoon together. The worms emit these substances from a small opening under their jaws, called the spinneret, as they spin. The two streams harden upon contact with air. When the spinning is completed, the worm's peanut-sized cocoon is covered with 300 to over 1,800 yards of filament.

If the cocoons are left undisturbed, a moth will emerge in about two weeks. However, this breaks the filaments into small pieces which makes the silk worthless. So unless the chrysalis has been

selected for breeding, the cocoons are steamed or heated to suffo-
cate the chrysalis or subjected to an ultrasonic whistle, procedures
which leave the filaments intact. The sericin, which is the cocoon's
cement, must be softened by repeated immersions in hot and cold
water in order for the silk to be unwound. This is done by hand. The
filaments of six cocoons are reeled together to form a strand finer
than a human hair, and six or eight of these strands are twisted into a
stronger yarn. Silk that still has a lot of gum in it is called raw silk, and
it remains hard and lusterless. The finer, soft and lustrous silks have
had their filaments boiled in soap and water to remove all the gum.

Silk is the most luxurious of fabrics; it is also the strongest
natural fiber. Because of its fineness and strength, it is a highly
desirable fabric for its durability. Because it is an animal fiber, it's
warmer than cotton or linen. Silken garments are absorbent so
perspiration does not leave the body clammy or damp. This makes
silk a perfect fabric for underwear and shirts. Silk prevents body heat
from radiating away from the body and, hence, it's desirable for
winter outerwear and scarves. Silk also makes fine, warm pajamas
and coat linings. However, because of its durability, silk can be
woven into very fine, open-weave yarns which permit air to pass
through the weave. Many fine, cool summer clothes can be made
with this fabric.

Silk fibers are very elastic. They regain shape easily, resist
wrinkling, and take dyes very well. Silk is very pliable and supple
and has excellent drapability, as the beauty of Japanese kimonos
can attest. The fabric is considered to be hygienic because its
smoothness resists dirt, and most silks are easily cleaned.

Because of their fineness, silk garments require a bit more care
than cottons. Although silks are usually easily cleaned, care must be
used in laundering them with mild soaps. The garments should not
be wrung, because the fibers are weakened slightly when they're
wet. Mild bleaches may be used, and silks may be dry-cleaned. If a
garment is stained by water spots, repeated cleanings will usually
restore its original beauty.

Silk clothes do not shrink very much, and ironing restores them
to their original size — but caution must be used because silks are

sensitive to heat. They should be ironed damp with a warm iron. Silk resists mildew and moths, but should be protected from direct sunlight. Excessive perspiration can damage silk clothes and discolor and stain them. If the clothes are worn close to the skin, they should be washed or cleaned regularly.

Silk is usually more expensive than other natural fibers. This is, of course, an important consideration in purchasing silk clothing. However, because of its durability, beauty and healthfulness, it is worth its price in the long run. With proper care, silk garments can give the natural dresser years of wear, comfort, and a fine, fashionable look.

Wool

The Hermitage Museum in Leningrad is the proud possessor of a woolen rug that has been dated to a period between 500 and 300 B.C. It is the oldest known woolen article in existence today and proves that humans have used the fleece of sheep for thousands of years. In the fourth century B.C., Alexander the Great found the natives of India wearing woolen cloth. Primitive people killed wild sheep for food and used the pelts as body coverings, but by the first century A.D., shepherds discovered that sheep could be bred to improve their fleece and then sheared.

The first crossbred variety of sheep was the merino; by the Middle Ages, Spain, who declared it a capital offense to export a merino from that country, was producing fine woolen clothes. Soon after, England, France, and Germany imported Spanish merinos for sheep breeding, and they eventually shipped the breed to Australia where the finest wools are bred today.

The soft, fleecy coats of domesticated sheep, which are shorn and spun into yarn, are the result of selective breeding and care. The process of turning wool into fiber is costly. As a consequence, wool is more expensive than plant fibers.

Because the quality of wool fiber is determined by many factors — breeding, climate, food, and the health of the sheep among them — there are many geographical areas that are more suited to sheep raising than others. There are about forty breeds of sheep, and with all the crossbreeding, there are close to two hundred grades of sheep. Grading is an important consideration in the fleece's fineness and length.

The best wools come from merino sheep. These breeds are raised all over the world. The fibers are short but strong, fine, and elastic. The qualities of merino wool contribute to its superior warmth and spinning qualities. Class Two wools, mostly from Great Britain, are of very good quality, also strong, fine, and elastic. Class Three wools are smoother and more lustrous than Class Two and merino wools, but are less resilient and elastic. Class Four wools are from mongrel or half-breed sheep. These wools are the least elastic and the least desirable; they are used for inexpensive, low-grade clothes.

Wool is also classified by fleece or the age at which the wool is shorn from the sheep. Lamb's wool is of very fine quality. Hogget wool, a very desirable soft, resilient wool, is the first shearing clipped from a fourteen-month sheep. Wether wool is fleece taken after a first shearing and contains a lot of dirt. Other grades of fleece, those taken from dead or sick sheep, should not be used in clothing.

Shearing is done in the spring by skilled people who average up to two hundred sheep a day using electric clippers. The fleece is baled and sent to mills to be scoured to remove animal grease, manure, dirt, and burrs — a process in which the fleece is washed in warm water and washing soda.

Fleece grows in locks that are curly, a factor that is permanent in the fiber. The more convoluted the fiber, the more insulating the yarn once it is spun, because more air can be trapped between the fiber layers. The outer covering of the wool fiber, its cuticle, is composed of scales that are similar to our pores, which breathe. The scales, microscopic in size, may cause some people to itch from wool. There are processes that either remove the scales completely or coat the fibers with a resin and make the garments machine-washable and nonscratching.

Wool fibers have the least strength of the natural fibers but are the most resilient. The strength of the fibers may be increased by adding twists to the yarns. Wool is very elastic and relaxes back to shape after each wearing. It also wrinkles less than other natural fiber garments, and any wrinkles can be easily steamed out. Good wools are soft and comfortable to the touch.

Wool fibers do not conduct heat and therefore help the body to maintain a healthy 98.6-degree temperature. Because the scales and natural twists in the fiber create insulating air pockets, they give the garment more warmth. The natural dresser will find wool garments excellent for winter wear. Surprisingly, lightweight wools are comfortable for summer clothes because the wools are thermostatic — the flow of air is regulated through the fibers. For example, desert peoples wear woolen burnooses and caftans in 100-degree weather because the loose fit allows for free air circulation both through the fiber and around the body. This personal air conditioning helps them stay cool on the hottest of days.

Wool drapes beautifully on the body. In fact, no other fiber, either natural or man-made can compete with its drapability. It is at once both water repellent and absorbent. Its innate qualities allow it to shed water droplets from the surface; but if it becomes very wet, the wool will heat to the body temperature, providing comfort rather than becoming cold or clammy to the skin's surface.

Its natural flame retardancy is an important factor because wools needn't be treated with harmful chemicals to prevent flammability. Wools dye readily, and their natural textures are enhanced because they can be knitted, blended, and woven in so many interesting and dramatic patterns.

With proper care, clothing made with this most comfortable and comforting of natural fibers will last for years. The woolen rug discussed earlier had been preserved by natural refrigeration in the frozen wastes of Siberia. Woolens require frequent cleaning because they tend to retain odors, and dirt adheres to the fabric. Most wools can be laundered in cool water with a mild soap such as Woolite, if they are handled carefully. The soap should be rinsed out thoroughly so no traces remain on the fibers. Wools shrink and lose strength temporarily when wet. They should not be pulled or wrung while wet, rather they should be blotted and squeezed in a towel and spread out to the original shape on a towel-covered, flat surface to dry. Harsh bleaches should not be used, but some wools may be bleached with products such as Snowy or Clorox Two.

Wools shrink less when they are dry-cleaned, and some wools have been sanforized, preshrunk, or treated to some other kind of shrinkproofing. Labels should be read to judge which care is best for a particular garment. Wrinkles can be steam-pressed out of the cloth. Prolonged exposure to sunlight weakens wool, as does perspiration. It is usually not susceptible to mildew, but it is especially vulnerable to moth infestation. Careful storage of woolen garments in a drawer with cedar chips or in bags will help prevent this problem. Natural dressers should avoid using commercial moth-proofing compounds because they contain allergenic and carcinogenic substances, such as benzene. These products are not necessary if the clothes are kept clean and stored properly.

Animal-Hair Fibers

In deciding on a complete year-round wardrobe, the natural dresser may choose several types of animal-hair fibers to provide warmth and comfort in cold weather. The most common animal fibers used for clothing are camel's hair, mohair, cashmere, alpaca, vicuña, and angora rabbit hair. Like wool, hair fibers have a long history and include among them the most exclusive and luxurious textiles. They are often blended with wools to add strength and beauty. The hairs of certain animals have adapted to climates by providing much warmth with the added quality of lightness. Some animals are specially bred for their hairs, and others are beasts of burden. Consumers should be aware that certain types of hair added to wool blends are in insignificant quantities and may be of the lowest grade. Labels should be checked carefully to insure the blends contain the fine qualities of the animal fibers discussed below.

Camel's hair is used in coats, gloves, and sweaters as well as rugs and other goods. Because of the climate of the desert, with the constant fluctuations in temperature, the camel develops a protective hair covering which conducts neither heat nor cold and is water-repellent. During the spring, the animal sheds its hair in matted clumps, preparing for its new growth. All the hair is then gathered. If softer hairs are required, the animal is plucked of its down. The hair is then combed to separate the down. There are several grades of camel's hair; a coat made from the highest grade of 100 percent camel hair is quite expensive. Therefore, camel hairs are sometimes blended with wools to lower the cost but still provide a high-quality, warm garment.

Mohair comes from the Angora goats of Turkey, a breed which has been successfully cultivated in the United States. The fibers are very strong, resilient, smooth, and lustrous and range in length from six to twelve inches. Mohair is receptive to dyes and lends itself to many decorative effects. It shrinks less than wool; is wrinkle-resistant; and is used for suits, dresses, coats, and sweaters.

Cashmere goats are native to the Himalayas. They are short-legged, long-haired animals with a fine, soft underhair, which provides a warm and luxurious fiber for clothing. The goats are not sheared, but are combed by hand during shedding seasons. The animals also rub against shrubs to relieve themselves of the itching of molting, and these fibers are also collected for yarns. The amount of fiber produced from each animal is small — two to four ounces per year. Consequently, it takes the fleece of four to six goats to produce a sweater. Cashmere garments, needless to say, are very expensive; but their softness and warmth are highly desirable for making extremely lightweight and comfortable sweaters, dresses, coats, and jackets. They should be treated like delicate wools.

The llama, which is indigenous to mountainous areas of South America, is a camel-like animal that grows a coarse, brownish hair which can be blended with other animal hairs to produce exquisite natural colors. These blends are lightweight, highly insulative, wrinkle-resistant, colorfast, and very durable. They are used for coat fabrics.

The alpaca, a native of the Andes and a cousin of the llama, produces silky, strong, water-repellent fibers. This domesticated animal is bred for its fleece, which is as delicate and lustrous as silk, but even more durable. Alpacas are shorn of their fleece by hand in the spring. The hairs are sorted and baled. Some of the hairs reach a length of thirty inches and range in color from white to brown and black with a reddish brown variety that is most valued. Alpaca fleece is usually blended with the hair of llamas for a warm, light-weight fabric used in coats, jackets, and ponchos.

The vicuña, is a rare, wild animal that inhabits the Andes like its cousins, the alpaca and llama. Reaching a height of three feet, each seventy-five-pound vicuña yields a bit less than one-quarter of a pound of hair per year, and as many as forty animals are needed to produce one coat. Of all the known animal hairs, vicuña is the most luxurious and delicate, yet it is extremely resilient and elastic — desirable qualities of any natural fiber. The animal is now under the protection of government agencies in Bolivia and Peru, and attempts have been made to domesticate it so more of the fleece can be cultivated. Vicuña garments are very costly and should be handled with great care to insure a long-wearing life.

Angora rabbit hair is long, fine, and silky. It is difficult to spin into yarn, but is blended with wools to provide texture and light-weight warmth. The hairs may be dyed pastel colors, and the fibers are used primarily in sweaters, baby clothes, and mittens.

Garments made with animal hairs should be brushed regularly and — with the exception of mohair, cashmere, and angora, which may be hand-washed in cool water with a mild soap — should be dry-cleaned. Animal-hair clothes should be stored in a cool place during warm-weather months and should not be kept in plastic coverings that prevent them from breathing. With proper care, animal-hair garments can give many years of wear and comfort. It is also nice to note that these animals are not slaughtered for their coats. These animals are well cared for because the fineness of their hairs is determined by their proper cultivation and diets.

Rayon

Rayon fabrics are man-made fibers generated from re-formed plant fibers. They differ from other synthetics in that they are biodegradable.

Rayon evolved as a result of the nineteenth century experiments of Count Hilaire de Chardonnet, who was trying to create silk. De Chardonnet succeeded in producing cellulose fibers rather than animal ones and laid the groundwork for man-made fibers, which are quite flammable and very weak when wet. The cellulose used in the early processes was derived from either cotton seeds after they had been ginned, or from soft wood pulps. The spinning process of rayon filament closely resembles the natural spinning of the silkworm. However, rayon is called regenerated cellulosic fiber because the original cellulose is changed by chemical actions into another form, and then converted back to a purified cellulose in fiber form.

The cellulose pulp is first steeped in caustic sodas; then it is forced through a spinneret into sulfuric acids, which turn the cellulose into a long filament that hardens and is then stretched. The filament is either twisted into yarn; reeled into skeins; washed, bleached, and dried; or it is left untwisted and cut into eight-inch lengths, which are then spun like natural fibers.

Rayon is a versatile fabric and less expensive than natural fibers. It is half as strong as silk and much weaker than cotton or linen. It is not as resilient or elastic as wool or cotton. However, rayon conducts heat well, making it acceptable for some summer clothing. Spun rayon may be napped to make it usable for winter clothes because napping provides insulation. Rayon is more absorbent than cotton and linen, but less so than wool and silk.

Unfortunately, rayon tends to shrink readily and must be chemically treated to make it flame retardant. Rayon takes dyes well and because of its smooth surface, sheds dirt. Most rayon fabrics are susceptible to mildew but resistant to moths and perspiration.

Because of its absorbency, rayon may be used in underwear. While not as comfortable as natural fiber fabrics, rayon may be worn if cost is a consideration. In purchasing rayon, the consumer should read care and content labels carefully to insure the clothes are made from the highest-quality fibers that require the least care.

Some rayon fibers lend themselves to dressier fabrics. Rayon drapes across the body well and has a high luster that makes it acceptable for garments worn for special occasions. The natural dresser may wish to add one or two rayon items to the wardrobe if silk clothes are prohibitive.

Rayon is a product of highly specialized technology and is made with costly equipment and chemical manipulations. Although naturally based, rayon is subject to chemicals and caustic sodas, and the feel of the fabric can only simulate that of a natural fiber. There is nothing quite like the texture, durability, and feel of cottons, linens, wools, and silks.

A look at the heat conductivity and absorbency of natural fibers versus man-made fibers quickly reveals that wearing natural fibers is just more comfortable and, hence, more healthy than wearing synthetics.

A General Comparison of Natural Fibers and Man-Made Fibers

Comfort Factors

Fiber	Heat Conductivity	Absorbency
Linen	The best conductor of heat. Wonderful for warm-weather clothes.	Very absorbent and dries quickly. Good for warm-weather wear.
Cotton	Excellent conductor of heat. Different weaves are suitable for both winter and summer wear.	Highly absorbent. Allows for perspiration evaporation. Good for sportswear and for active people.
Silk	Light weaves excellent for warm-weather wear; heavier ones perfect for winter clothes.	Very absorbent and good for cool, damp days. Comfortable on hot days. Perspiration can evaporate freely.
Wool	Most insulative fiber for cool, cold, and wet weather.	Very absorbent and wonderfully comfortable on cold, wet days. Does not allow skin to get damp, allows perspiration to evaporate.
Rayon	Good heat conductor. Useful in summer clothing, particularly when blended with a a higher amount of natural fibers.	Absorbent, but garments get heavy and wet if the air is humid.

Fiber	Heat Conductivity	Absorbency
Acetate	Does not conduct heat well. Very uncomfortable in warm weather.	Unsuitable in warm weather. Keeps moisture in, and wearer feels clammy and wet. Perspiration cannot evaporate from body.
Nylon	Peculiarly warm in summer and cool in winter.	Very unabsorbent, particularly in warm, humid weather. Fabrics do not dry quickly and can feel very clammy on humid days. Perspiration does not evaporate freely from the body.
Acrylics and Modacrylics	Can be too warm for cool weather wear, but unsuitably warm for summer wear. Children and infants can overheat in hot weather in these garments.	Similar to nylon and uncomfortable. Perspiration evaporation is limited.
Polyesters	Fair conductors of heat. Must be blended with natural fibers to be comfortable.	Water repellent, but not absorbent. Unless blended with a natural fiber, can be very clammy. Does not let perspiration evaporate freely.
Spandex	Holds heat in the body. Very uncomfortable in warm weather and for active people in any climate.	Nonabsorbent. Does not let perspiration evaporate freely.
Saran and Polypropelene	Holds heat in the body. Unacceptable in warm climates.	Nonabsorbent. Perspiration does not evaporate.

5

The body is not just a hanger for clothes

Many external environmental factors are deleterious to our health. But what about our internal environments? What diseases are caused by how we live? The largest killer in this country is heart disease. Are coronary problems environmental — caused by what we breathe? Or are they caused by how we breathe — the stress factors of daily life?

What does this have to do with clothing? In the first place, clothing bears heavily on how our bodies are restricted and constricted. Belts are worn to tighten and hold up skirts and pants. But belts can constrict breathing, lessen the amount of oxygen flow to the bloodstream, and subsequently increase feelings of stress. Similarly, ties and tight collars contribute to cutting off oxygen flow. People loosen their belts after a big meal, or open their collars if they really have to get work done. They are freeing themselves of their culturally induced constrictions. They know they must breathe in order to feel comfortable as they work or digest their food.

Breathing is essential in stress situations. Athletes require quick breaths (hyperventilations) to raise their oxygen intake in order to perform feats of strength and speed; women in childbirth are encouraged to pant to increase the air flow as they go through the contractions of labor. When people relax, they inhale and exhale deeply. None of these are possible if our bodies are bound up, and our chests and abdomens restricted from expanding to their fullest.

If the breath is not utilized properly and each breath taken is shallow, we cannot rely on deep breathing to sustain us in stressful situations. Stressful situations cause strong visceral reactions — shoulders tighten, bodies stiffen, breath becomes shallow and more labored. This can lead to increased tension, and finally to total distress — a syndrome that throws the body completely off balance and into a danger zone where muscles weaken and strength rapidly leaves the body. The heart cannot withstand this strain and often suffers an attack at this point.

Although we may not be in immediate danger of heart attacks from restrictive clothing, we may be slowly suffocating ourselves by tightening our clothes with belts, girdles, tight pants, and skirts. Our culture encourages us to "suck in our stomachs," to slenderize ourselves artificially by girdles, to truss ourselves up in ties and high collars, and to take up the slack of clothes in much the same way the boa tightens around its hapless prey.

In order to dress for health, we must be aware of our body and how it functions. We must be aware that tight clothing can interfere with our body's most important processes: breathing, circulation, and digestion. We must also be aware that the body is a magnificent piece of architecture that provides structural supports from which to hang clothes that can drape and enhance our bodies, instead of interfere with them.

Respiration

Correct breathing is extremely important in order for us to have a vital, alive body. The rate of regularity of this oxygenization has important effects on the various organs. Dr. Rudolph Ballentine, author of *Science of Breath,* puts this quite elegantly: "The rhythm of the breath creates rhythmic waves of energy that wash the body like the waves of the ocean breaking upon the seashore."

Balance in respiration is the key to optimize the rate and rhythm of oxygenation, which in turn energizes the tissues. If breathing is obstructed by a tight belt around the diaphragm area, a tight brassiere around the chest or thoracic region, or a collar band constricting the clavicular area, there is an increase of carbon dioxide in the blood and a decrease in oxygen. The obstruction may be great or slight, but even a slight change may cause the body suffering. Without the correct exchange balance between the gases of breathing (oxygen and carbon dioxide), wastes accumulate and become a constant irritant. This same tension can cause a build-up of wastes in muscle tissue, which results in stress and pain. If this happens, a decrease in alertness will occur, which can lead to depression or sluggishness.

The mechanisms for breathing, the chest and abdomen, are contained in the torso of the body. The two sections are separated by a large muscle called the diaphragm, which forms the floor of the chest cylinder. The chest is rigid and reinforced by the ribs in which are contained the lungs. Upon an inhalation the chest reaches its maximum capacity when the diaphragm is pulled taut or flattened. During exhalation, the diaphragm becomes dome-shaped, and the volume of the chest cavity is reduced by the pressure of the abdominal organs.

The abdomen, on the other hand, is not rigid; its front wall can expand and contract freely. There are four abdominal muscles that greatly aid breathing. These flatten the belly and push its contents up to the chest during exhalation. On inhaling, the diaphragm contracts as the belly relaxes. This is a bit like a massage, with gentle pressure and relaxation in one direction and then another. This massage helps the functions of the other body organs, particularly the intestines, aiding in digestion. Any clothing that obstructs or interferes with this rhythm not only hurts the efficiency of the breathing organs, but is harmful to the body in general.

In a normal breathing state, we use the mechanism that requires the least effort and establishes the most harmonious rhythm. This diaphragmatic breathing requires very little muscular exertion on the part of the body. Too many of us suffer from shallow breathing because the fashions we wear do not permit the natural mechanisms of our bodies to perform properly. If a belt or button is too tight, we tend to gasp for air rather than loosen the clothes. After a period of time, we can adapt to this shallow breathing which causes the whole system to dysfunction. This is a serious situation. Breathing is the source of life and nothing should be done to interfere with its natural function. Clothing worn on the body's torso should be loose and allow the muscles to expand and contract freely.

Circulation

William Harvey, a great Renaissance physician, teacher, and researcher "discovered" the human circulatory system in 1528. Through intensive experimentation coupled with deductive reasoning and logic, he found that blood flows from the heart through the aorta and branching arteries to the parts of the body and then flows back to the heart through the veins. Dr. Harvey proclaimed that our hearts are the center of our personal universes. "The animal's heart is the basis of its life, its chief member, the sum of its microcosm, on the heart all its activities depend, from the heart all its liveliness and strength arise." This simple statement describes the most important function of the body: the flow of life-giving, oxygenated blood, circulating throughout a closed system.

Drs. Michael de Bakey and Antonio Gorro of National Heart and Blood Vessel Research and Demonstration Center at Baylor College of Medicine, Houston, Texas, developed an interesting metaphor for the circulatory system in their book *The Living Heart.*

Think of the body as a continent packed with billions of people, the equivalent of the cells that make up a human being. Without adequate nourishment and sanitation, these billions will die and the continent will become lifeless. A steady flow of trucks, represented by the blood stream, carry oxygen, water and foodstuffs to the cells and haul away waste over 60,000 miles of roadway, the extent of the blood vessels in a normal adult.

The trucks with fresh loads of oxygen and foodstuffs begin their trips from the heart over a broad one-way highway, known as the aorta. Slightly smaller avenues (arteries) branch off into the countryside and these, in turn, subdivide into arterioles. These roadways are capable of widening themselves when some area of the body requires more supplies quickly. Finally, one arrives at the capillaries, alleys so narrow that just a single vehicle, or blood cell, visible only under a powerful microscope, can squeeze through. Nestled in the spaces between cellular tissues, the capillaries deliver the food and oxygen to the ultimate consumer, the cell. Simultaneously, waste is collected. Following the deliveries and collections, the blood cells leave nitrogen wastes in the kidneys, and carbon dioxide in the lungs for disposal. (Urination by the former, exhalation the latter.) Oxygen is loaded on in the lungs and other materials are gathered from the stomach, liver and endocrine glands, adipose (fatty) tissue and other organs. (p. 15)

To carry this metaphor a bit further, how unfortunate that we, the owners of this marvelously efficient system of supply and demand often obstruct, disconnect, in fact hijack the processes by our clothing.

Pressure stops or at least slows blood flow. How dangerous wearing a tight belt around the diaphragm area of the body can be, not only to breathing but to circulation — literally, it stanches the blood flow! Additionally, tight, restrictive trousers or pants — particularly jeans, which are designed (or expected) to be worn too tight — may apply tourniquet-type pressure to the groin area preventing the proper flow of blood to the upper legs, calves, and feet. Also, any clothing that restricts muscular activity in any way may, in turn, obstruct venous activity, particularly in the legs.

Poor circulation can lead to a myriad of ills, running the gamut from phlebitis to coronary thrombosis, with varicose veins, hemorrhoids, strokes, nephritis, and hypertension in between. Unfortunately, much of our health activity is geared toward the alleviation of symptoms, not the prevention of illness. Clothing can be a measure to help prevent many illnesses, particularly any that are caused by poor circulation, notably edema, or swelling, and varicose veins.

Digestion and Body Harmony

Because all the parts of the body work in harmony, the circulatory system plays as essential a role in the function of digestion as do the respiratory organs. Anything that obstructs the flow of blood or oxygen hampers digestion. Additionally, the stomach must be allowed freedom to perform its function, as must the small intestines and large intestines, which are encased in the abdominal area. Undue pressure from tight clothes exerted in this area hampers digestion.

The gastrointestinal tract's activity is truly remarkable from the moment food is taken into the mouth through the time it is eliminated through the colon. The movement of materials through the system is called peristalsis, which is a wavelike, muscular contraction. Although digestive activity is initiated and controlled by the autonomic nervous system, digestion may be voluntarily aided by eating habits, exercise and physical activity, and keeping the body relaxed and comfortable in clothing that allows it to function normally.

Genitourinary System

The functions of the genitourinary tracts, the organs of reproduction and elimination, of both males and females are involuntarily controlled by the autonomic nervous system. However, like digestion, these systems may be hampered or abetted by our voluntary actions.

The primary male sexual organs are housed outside the body in the scrotum. These organs consist of the testes, producers of the male hormone testosterone and of spermatozoa. Liquid waste, urine, is collected by the kidneys and stored in the bladder before excretion. This is eliminated through an opening in the penis. The female genitourinary tract is basically internal, with the reproductive organs protected within the pelvic girdle and abdominal wall. However, the vaginal and urethral openings, often the site of infection and irritation, are exposed to direct contact with wearing apparel.

In both men and women chafing of external genitalia may be a serious problem. Any area that is constantly rubbed by an article of clothing may develop a sore or raw patch that is subject to additional irritation from laundry detergents and chemicals in the clothing themselves. Skin absorbs some chemicals readily from fabrics; if the skin is broken, the possible risk of a harmful substance entering the body is increased. This is an important concern in the genital area. If clothes are kept in tight contact with the area and rubbed continuously against the skin, severe damage may be done to the tissue and underlying organs.

Women in particular are susceptible to many problems. Some dyes used in pantyhose cause dermatitis. Panties, jeans, and trousers may also contain these dyes, and the chemicals may invade the delicate tissues of the vagina. Some women find that tight underwear and jeans cause them much discomfort if they have any type of genitourinary tract infections, such as vaginitis or cystitis. Treatment of these conditions involves keeping the area clean, dry, free from irritants, and covered by cotton panties which allow perspiration to evaporate.

It may be worthwhile to recommend preventive rather than palliative measures. In this case it would mean wearing loose-fitting, undyed (or vegetable-dyed), natural-fiber garments which allow normal bacteria to thrive in a healthy environment, rather than fabrics that don't breathe and remain damp from perspiration. It is also a good idea to avoid clothing that binds the crotch area and prevents healthy blood circulation.

The Architecture of the Body

Clothing that is too tight will hamper respiration, digestion, and circulation. It will also hamper freedom of movement and increase muscular tension. The architecture of the body is such that a clothing designer can choose to allow healthy freedom of movement, while utilizing the marvelous structural support that the skeleton provides.

Muscles

There are over six hundred voluntary muscles in the human body. These, under the conscious control of the brain, give us a variety of movements and actions. In order for actions to be carried out in a strong, rhythmic, balanced fashion, the muscles must be kept in condition by exercise and good nutrition. But the external care of muscles through proper attire may be just as important in allowing them to carry out their functions.

Ben Benjamin, author of *Are You Tense?* claims that faulty habits may be prime causes of muscular tension. Among these, he describes wearing tight clothing and high-heeled shoes as mechanical sources of tension. Muscular tension has a serious effect on breathing and blood circulation. The primary muscle for breathing is the diaphragm, which can be strained by tension caused by belts, brassieres, pants, and ties. In a vicious circle, tension prevents us from breathing properly, and not breathing properly makes us tense. This tension can be greatly relieved just by loosening clothes.

Tension in muscles may also restrict blood circulation. This can happen if the muscles contract around blood vessels. Many of us, in an effort to be in fashion, wear clothing that is too small. Clothes that are too small apply constant pressure to the abdomen, waist, lower-back area, and the diaphragm. Strain is placed on muscles if we wear styles that distort the body's true shape, such as constantly sucking abdominal muscles in to wear skin-tight jeans; pushing breasts upward with bras; and binding the muscles of the legs in pants, trousers, and boots with circumferences smaller than that of the leg.

An increase of lactic acid in the tissues can be caused by strain. This may cause extreme pain and discomfort. An obvious example of this kind of strain is wearing high heels for too long. The muscles can become incapable of responding to nerve impulses, or they can become overly tense and unable to relax. Often they lose tone as a result of too much tension.

Skeletal System

The spine, a column of small bones held together by ligaments, is the fundamental basis of support and movement for the human body. A cushion-like substance called cartilage lies between each layer, and the spinal cord, which contains many of the body's major nerves, runs through the column. The spine, or backbone as it is sometimes called, is very flexible and allows for all body movements. The spine divides the body into two canals: the ventral (visceral), which houses all the vital organs, and the dorsal (neural), which contains the central nervous system.

The skeleton has been called nature's mechanical triumph because it balances the forces of nature and helps us move. But the skeleton is not just the originator of motion. It forms protection for the major organs and supports and bears the weight of the body.

The shoulder is a yoke-like structure. It is connected to the spine only through the sternum, which is attached to the ribs. The shoulder supports the arms and enables them to move freely and powerfully without causing pressure in the chest. The shoulder protects respiratory, circulatory, and nervous system functions. The bones are strong and designed for efficiency and comfort of the body.

Mabel Todd, the author of *The Thinking Body* says, "If allowed free play, the shoulder girdle gives the best balance, as it maintains its balance more effectively in motion." It gives support to the head and the spine. She suggests that the motion of the shoulder should not be hampered by being held rigidly up and back as this interferes with the motion of the clavicle and throws off the whole alignment of the ribs and sternum which ultimately disorients the thoracic region of the body. This may severely hamper breathing mechanisms.

Clothing — such as tight-sleeved jackets, shirts, or dresses and tight over-the-shoulder bra straps, ties, corsets, and girdles — can hamper the shoulder area significantly enough to cause a dangerous structural imbalance in the body which can result in pain, stress, and strain. Todd explains, " . . . any force operating upon an object induces some degree of stress within, since no action can occur without a reaction," and "every stress within a structure threatens its integrity by altering the cohesion of its molecules. If the stress continues beyond the ability of the substance to resist, the structure will give way."

However, parts of the body need not be deformed for them to be strained. Strain may be cumulative; it may take years before a change is noticeable. Wearing uncomfortable, tight clothing may not do immediate damage, but over a period of time, during which the body has overcompensated for its discomfort and structurally misaligned itself, the strain may show severely.

The pelvis is brilliantly designed to provide weight support and movement to the body. It is a light structure containing many openings since a solid bone with legs attached would be prohibitively heavy for the body to bear. Three bones make up the structure; the illium, the ischium, and the pubes. The male's pelvis falls backward and the female's forward. The female's pelvis is wider, with a shallower groin area and broader sacrum. It's puzzling that women have been encouraged to wear men's jeans when their physical structure is so clearly different from men's. In actuality, these clothes cannot comfortably fit women's bodies.

The skeletal system is very strong and flexible. It provides a wonderful framework not only for the body, but for points of support for our clothes. Rather than fasten clothing across the body, binding, chafing, and putting tight pressure on the organs in the process, we can use the structure of the bones to provide a framework for hanging the clothes from structural points, such as the shoulder and the pelvis. In this way, dressing can flow with the body's architecture rather than harm it.

Artists and sculptors study anatomy in order to understand drapery and clothing flow across the body's lines. The body is a three-dimensional form with height, width, and depth. Clothing is designed from a two-dimensional perspective; but what looks good on paper just may not work on the body. Freedom of movement is ensured by loose-fitting, comfortably designed, and proportioned clothes. Perhaps more importantly, these types of clothes allow a certain freedom of movement *within* the body as well, permitting the system to work at its peak efficiency and allowing the body to regulate itself, promoting health and well-being. Later we provide ideas and blueprints for clothing that flows and drapes over the natural architecture of the body. These are clothes that look good *and* feel good on the body.

6

Feet and our bodies' foundation

Too often we view our feet as mere appendages of the body — at the very bottom of both the whole organism and of our care-priority list. But when our feet hurt, we can't feel good anywhere. In fact, foot comfort is so important to our health that a whole chapter can be devoted to it.

Modern urban dwellers usually do most of their walking on a hard surface, either concrete or asphalt. Few of us get the opportunity to do much walking on sand, grassy land, or even dirt roads. These terrains offer a kind of natural massage to a bare foot, help exercise foot joints, and provide a sound, soft base on which the body can stand. People were once able to go barefoot because the earth's surface was unpaved. The feet toughened and calloused as a result of contact with the earth and formed natural protection against cuts and bruises. With the development of pavement came the necessity for wearing shoes to protect feet from the hard surfaces.

If shoes complement feet they are not detrimental in themselves. In fact, if they don't bind the feet or cut into the toes or prevent flexibility, they can be quite comfortable. However, for some reason, civilized people have always had a need to reform the foot in some way either by binding or squashing it or by deforming the angles of its bones by a hard, ungiving structure. The general tendency of stylish, western footwear is to confine and restrict the foot's movement. However, like other parts of the body, the foot must be permitted to expand and contract, to breathe, and to dissipate moisture in order for it to be healthy.

Humans are upright animals, and their arms and legs are proportionally larger than those of the closest primate relatives. To support the upright posture and heavy limbs, human feet touch the ground at the ball and heel, providing a base to distribute weight evenly. The foot acts as a lever, strong enough to withstand body propulsion as well as support it while standing still. Our feet bear the responsibility of supporting our entire bodies, unique in the animal kingdom.

There are twenty-six bones in each foot. The bones are held together by ligaments, and muscles form an arch. The muscles support and strengthen the arch. As with any other body part, if the muscles and ligaments are kept strong, the foot functions properly.

Footwear should complement our feet, not replace the function of our muscles or hinder them. They should not make the function of the foot obsolete, but rather be protection against rough terrain, helpers that enable us to adapt to our surroundings. A healthy foot does its job of support very well. It does not need to be redesigned by shoe styles. Just because we've managed to replace living earth with concrete, we needn't seek to replace our feet with corresponding structures that inhibit natural functions.

Footwear

The beginnings of shoes are hard to trace. In all probability, feet were originally covered by animal furs wrapped around them. People in warmer climates wore sandals made from plant fibers and leather. As with clothing, shoes soon became decorative and descriptive of social class. The social aspects of what people wear on their feet are as varied as what people put on their backs. For some reason feet have been eroticized. Perhaps this can be traced to ancient Rome where a bare foot was the mark of wantonness, and only a prostitute would go unshod. In fact, a woman's desirability could be determined by the sight of her foot: ladies always covered their feet, however diaphanously or sparsely.

By the Middle Ages, the poulaine, an extremely pointed shoe, was very much in vogue in Europe. This phallic-shaped shoe was the focus of embittered moral battles; despite the clergy's ban on wearing them, they were still popular as late as the eighteenth century. The length of the toe points of these shoes often reached two feet and had to be supported by whalebones. Sometimes the ends were tied up around the leg. Both men and women found it difficult to walk in poulaines, but the courts of Europe treasured the silly things regardless.

Modern poulaines have peaked in a new form: an extremely high-heeled, wooden-platformed, slip-on shoe for women. These shoes have a colorful, Anglo-Saxon vernacular nomenclature, which suggests to some people a kind of sexual congress. Men do not wear these seduction shoes, but they allegedly are "turned on" by them. Could it be said the Age of the Foot Fetish has arrived?

As popular as poulaines might have been in the twelfth century, they could not compete with the ubiquity of today's jogging shoes, from which future generations might determine that we were a race of shoe fetishists. Because of the national phenomenon of running, feet are finally getting some attention from shoe manufacturers and medical practitioners alike. It's possible that out of the work and study done on our newly athletic feet, a new awareness of healthy shoes for all aspects of life will emerge. Maybe then we'll put our twentieth century poulaines in the museum, or the garbage can, where they belong.

The Problems with Shoes

One of the major causes of backaches is improper heel height. The upright body must force the shoulders back and the pelvis out in order to balance in heels higher than two inches, although the negative effects of higher heels can be offset a bit by wearing a thicker platform on the ball of the foot.

Overly high heels can also distort the shape of the foot, put stress on the tendons by stretching the ones in front and shortening the ones in back, particularly the Achilles tendon. Then, if shorter heels are worn, the Achilles tendon may cramp. Much stress is placed on the toes when the foot is pushed forward in a high-heeled shoe and a callus may form on the ball of the foot from the continued pressure. The combination of high heels and pointed-toe shoes push the foot forward and compress it, squeezing the toe bones together. If the nerves between these bones become irritated, a neuroma (or nerve tumor) may develop.

It's been said that high heels were invented by a woman who had been kissed on the forehead, surely a chauvinistic view at best. Most probably high heels were invented by someone who knew how to make a buck and saw lots of them in fashion whims. High heels can be dangerous and unhealthy for the feet and body. Certainly most styles are uncomfortable, but for many of our current western fashions, high heels are important to make the lines of the garment fall properly. Also, physical stature is admired in our culture. A tall, slim body is encouraged. Adult women are told to add two inches to their height when measuring themselves up against standardized height and weight charts. It's a national assumption that a woman will wear heels all the time, and therefore she can just add two inches to her needy legs. In our culture, high heels are the prosthetic devices of people who are viewed as permanently crippled by their lack of height.

An intelligent, if not altogether healthy, compromise could be to wear high heels when an occasion calls for it, but to change heel heights during the day to ensure that leg muscles and tendons get a proper stretch. However, it is recommended that a lower heel be worn most of the time because it's best for the whole body.

Aside from distortions caused by pointed toes and high heels, other shoe shapes may be just as dangerous. Square-toed shoes in no way conform to the shape of the foot. Additionally, if the sole of the shoe is narrower than the sole of the foot, permanent creases may occur on the sole and so may soft corns between the toes. One of the reasons why women seem to suffer from more foot problems than men may be caused by the tremendous variety of shoe styles available to them — styles that do not conform to the foot's natural flexibility and that constrict nerves and skin as well as distort the shape of the toes.

Any shoe, improperly fitted, may result in poor circulation. Poor circulation may cause edema (swelling), tissue anoxia, arteriosclerosis, and varicose veins.

Circulatory diseases of the feet may be caused by restrictive and tight clothes worn on the body as well as by tight shoes and hosiery. Tissue anoxia is a lack of oxygen caused by an inadequate blood supply to the legs. Anything that hampers the blood supply in the torso, arms, and legs will eventually affect the feet.

Care should be taken at every stage of life to ensure proper fit of shoes to avoid any circulation constriction. Special consideration must be given to older people and diabetics who are particularly susceptible to circulatory diseases.

Many other serious foot problems are caused by poorly fitted shoes. Among these are corns, bunions, and calluses. There are two types of corns: soft, which are usually found between the toes where they become rubbery from the moisture of the foot; and hard, which develop over the toe joints. Corns are quite painful when pressure is applied, but some hurt all the time. The corns that develop on joints may progress further into the joints and inflame the fluid sacs that lubricate the joints. This causes bursitis. The prime culprit in corn development is the pointed-toed shoe. If shoes rub against toes, corns may develop, usually at the place the shoe rubs the foot.

Calluses are a thickening of the skin, usually on the sole of the foot. They are often caused by the pressure placed on the ball of the foot by the angle and height of the heel. A way to treat calluses is to remove the weight pressure on the ball of the foot by lowering the height of the heels worn.

Bunions are enlarged fluid sacs (bursas) in the joint of the big toe. This may cause a severe angulation and distortion of the toe known as Hallux Valgus. The joint may become swollen and hurt severely. This condition is usually caused by squeezing the toes together in any unnatural shape. High heels also contribute by placing excess weight and pressure on the big toe's joint. Bunions are extremely serious and may totally displace the other bones of the feet.

Ingrown toenails are caused by the nail growing down and into the flesh on the sides of the nail. This inflames the skin and may cause infection. The major cause of this condition is the tight shoe. Tight socks or stockings may also contribute to the problem.

Finally, feet are often attacked by fungal infections, the most common of which is athlete's foot or ringworm. This condition is not really caused by wearing ill-fitting shoes, but may be controlled and aided by wearing shoes that breathe and allow air to circulate around the foot. Proper hygiene is a tremendous factor — clean socks and hosiery should always be worn.

Better Shoes for Better Living

Better shoes for better living begins with buying shoes that fit properly. Proper fit means that there is no pressure on the toes or the ball of the foot. The heel of the shoe should fit the heel of the foot and not rub against the Achilles tendon. The front of the shoe should give room for the toes to move. The shoe sole should be able to bend without binding the toes. The only place the shoe should be snug is in the arch and across the instep.

As for shoe designs — while it may not be entirely feasible to return to primitive man's shoes of wrapped furs and sandals, it might be a good idea to consider some of their healthier aspects. For example, feet should be wrapped in a fashion that does not obstruct circulation in cold weather. Sandals are a good idea for warm weather.

In warm weather a sandal is ideal because it reduces heat transfer from the ground and allows cooling air to flow over the tops of the feet. Additionally, sandals allow space for all the toes, and allow the feet to breathe and disperse perspiration. If exposure to the sun must be avoided, absorbent, light cotton socks should be worn. The feet must always be kept clean and dry, however, to avoid fungal infections.

For wet weather when boots must be worn, canvas allows less sweat to accumulate than leather. Wool or cotton socks should be worn for comfort, warmth, and perspiration dispersal. As with all other clothing, shoes and socks must breathe. Plastics and vinyl materials do not allow this and should not be worn on the feet. Canvas and leather breathe and adjust to the feet. They also stretch and can be made into better-fitting shoes than the plastics and vinyls.

There are healthy shoes. The Birkenstock Shoe Company makes a very healthy and comfortable sandal based on the idea that in order for a shoe to fit properly it must conform to the imprint of the individual foot. In their literature, Birkenstock suggests that people wear fashion shoes as often as necessary, but wear Birkenstock footwear as often as possible. This is sensible advice since these sandals are handsome, and, when properly fitted, can give years of service and comfort to the feet. The heel is balanced with the toes and helps to distribute body weight properly.

Shakti is the yogic word for energy, and Shakti Shoes claim to massage and stimulate the energy flow through the feet. These shoes have a contoured footbed, and the heel and toes are balanced like the Birkenstocks to distribute weight evenly. This also contributes to good posture. Shakti shoes cover the whole foot in good leather and provide good support through the heel and ankles. They're great for walking, look good, and give excellent wear.

The Cordwainers of Deerfield, New Hampshire, are a family of shoe makers who design and make stylish, comfortable, and healthy shoes. Cordwainer Creations, as they are called, are made to order and hence are more expensive than store-bought shoes, but there's absolutely no comparison between the two. These attractive shoes are made to fit *your* feet and *your* toes, not standardized versions of them. The Cordwainers express concern for proper circulation and for foot exercise. Their shoes demonstrate this concern by their flexibility, attention to fit, and the use of all natural materials. The shoes can be repaired in their factory and carry a three-year warranty.

The shoes we've mentioned are excellent examples of healthy ideas for footwear. All of them require an outline of the individual's foot to ensure proper sizing when purchased by mail order, and the shoes are sold in carefully selected outlets. In surveying other types of shoes, we have found some have good aspects in some shoes, but often not in all. It is essential for health that people wear several types of shoes, change them often, but most importantly, make sure the fit is correct.

7

A holistic view of health and dressing

The means whereby man is created, the means whereby disease occurs, the means whereby man is cured, the means whereby disease arises: The Meridians are the basis of all theory and treatment.

Ling Shu

For a long time we have let the medical establishment completely define health and health care. As a result, Americans' view of health has been allopathic, derived mainly from the point of view of curing diseases, not preventing illness. And the cures have been mostly technological in concept — drugs, biomedical machines, intricate surgery. These techniques separate parts of the body from the whole and treat each as an unrelated entity. Recently a new way of looking at health has evolved, a way which views the human body in relation to the environment and which views all parts of the body in relation to each other and the entire system. It is called holistic health. In this chapter we will examine some of the principles of holistic health to see how it relates to dressing for health.

Meridian Flow

The Oriental idea of healing is based on a concept of energy passing through meridians of the body. These channels of energy are called meridian lines; each is named for a corresponding organ in the body. Meridian lines are divided into two forces — yin and yang. Yin lines flow upward starting at the toes and moving through the center of the body to the head and fingertips. Yang lines flow downward, starting at the fingertips and the top of the head and descending down through the center of the body. There are six yin meridians and six yang meridians. Three meridians flow in each arm and leg. Two other meridians run along the front and back of the body. Meridians connect the organs, limbs, and muscles of the body. This concept is important because of its holistic view of the body. Pain in a particular area may signify that another part along that meridian is ill. In Oriental health treatments, different points along one meridian are stimulated either by pressure, as in shiatsu, or by needles, as in acupuncture.

The types of clothing worn to cover these areas should be chosen carefully. They should neither pinch nor chafe; the fabrics should be soft and provide breathability for the skin; and no particular area should receive more stimulation or pressure than another — to do so might throw off the delicate balance of the body's energy flow.

The feet play a very special role in this energy flow. Mythology tells us that the ancient Greek warrior Antaeus was invincible as long as he touched the earth, his mother. Although we may not be godlike wrestlers, we experience a connection with Mother Earth through our feet, one which can strengthen us, as it did Antaeus, and add to our health. Cosmic energy emanates from the planet and is transmitted to our bodies through the feet. The vibratory messages received by the body are determined not only by the surface of the terrain, but also by the condition of our feet, either healthy or unhealthy. Similarly, the body's organs, which have nerve endings in the feet, are affected by the same things.

Just as walking on swampland will produce different messages to the nerves and brain from walking on desert sand, so too will wearing one type of shoe produce different feelings from wearing another. Anything that interferes with a healthy transmission of vibrations, gravity, cosmic energy, or the vital life force, which the yogis call prana, may prove in the long run to be quite detrimental to health. Since the feet are the foundations of this earth and body relationship, the kinds of foot coverings we wear are extremely important.

Fig. 7–1. *This diagram shows the areas of the foot that correspond to specific organs of the body.*

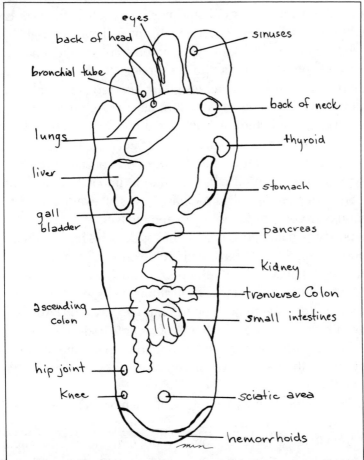

Perhaps it can be viewed in this way: the surface or skin of the earth transmits rhythms and feelings to the skin of our bodies through the soles of the feet. Just as the food chain is a continuous circle of the life from nourished soil, through plants, animals, humans, and back to the soil again, the energy chain of cosmic forces sends vibrations through our bodies, and, with the help of gravity, back to the earth again.

Foot reflexology, acupuncture, and shiatsu tell us that each bodily organ has extremely sensitive nerve endings in the feet. Reflexologists diagram the feet as miniature bodies with each part of the foot representing a corresponding organ of the body: the toes refer to the head, ears, eyes, and nose; the ball of the foot corresponds to the liver, pancreas, stomach, and gall bladder; right below the arch represents the kidney, transverse colon, and small intestines; and the sole under the heel refers to the sexual organs. Additionally, the ovaries and testes are affected at the ankle of the left foot, the sciatic nerve runs through the Achilles tendon, the prostate gland and uterus are affected at the inside right ankle, and the bladder point is located at the inner right arch. If these foot areas are the victims of tight, ill-fitted shoes and constant pressure, the body may be thrown off balance and put into spasm and pain.

Shiatsu specialist Wataru Ohashi gives an example of the correlation between a diseased organ and the feet. ". . . Find someone with poor vision and press hard in the inside of his big toe, the part of the foot where the eyes have their nerve endings. He will probably scream with pain . . . " Pity the poor people with bad vision! The constant pinching of their toes by ill-fitting shoes may keep them in a constant state of agony, discomfort, and aggravation. Almost anyone would agree, if your feet hurt, your whole body feels miserable. Ohashi claims that if there is "exceptional pain and stiffness . . . anywhere in the foot, the organ represented by that area is having trouble."

Viewing the body as a whole, with each part affecting the other, and seeing that there is a constant interchange of energy from side to side, front to back, top to bottom, it is not difficult, indeed it appears necessary, to treat the system as a whole with each part relating significantly to the next. Providing a comfortable outer covering for the body can only help this system maintain its balance and health.

Life Cycles

All the energy of the universe flows in cycles; these too affect our well-being. The cycles include the lunar (the phases of the moon), which controls the tides; solar, which controls weather, sunrises, and sets; and the growth of plants and animals. Planetary (zodiacal) cycles affect the weather and seasons and may also affect individuals born under their conjuncts and signs. Primitive peoples were much more conscious of the effects of these natural cycles and based their religions as well as their lifestyles on the patterns of the moon, sun, and planets.

As integral parts of the energy of the universe, our bodies are affected by these cycles. Also, each individual organism has its own life cycle. Within this life cycle, there are eating, sleeping, and sexual cycles, which should not be treated lightly if the body is to remain in a healthy state. Just as each person is different from the next, so too are individual cycles unique; each person must find out his or her own. For example, although most normal women experience a monthly menstrual cycle beginning at the age of about twelve and lasting for approximately forty years, each woman's experience of her period differs from the next.

It is becoming increasingly obvious that men also experience a kind of sexually oriented cycle. This is not marked as is a woman's passage of blood, but may be as strong in emotional, physical, and spiritual ways as a woman's. Unfortunately, our culture for generations has not allowed males to express emotions freely. As we expand our horizons to understand the power of these cycles, both male and female, we will not only learn more about ourselves as living beings, but more about living.

All of us share in the cycles of eating and sleeping, and each of us has an individual pattern. In as regimented world as we live in today, it becomes difficult to ferret out exactly what these patterns are. If one holds a nine-to-five job, eating and sleeping will have to coincide with this time schedule. However, individuals often have different requirements from each other. One of the reasons why people are obese may be because they are trying to conform to a rigid schedule that forces them to eat when they are not hungry, eventually disorienting their own appetites and confusing their systems into hunger patterns prescribed by unnatural, albeit socially beneficial, living conditions.

This may also affect those who are too thin by enforcing a timetable unnatural to their systems. They may not be able to eat at a prescribed time because of a lack of hunger. Later they may not be able to eat because of a lack of time. In both cases, people are often forced to eat too quickly to really enjoy a nourishing, health-sustaining meal.

Sleeping cycles, too, vary among individuals. Some people can get by with four or five hours of sleep a night, while others require ten or twelve hours to be fully alert. Still others need naps during the day or prefer to sleep in shifts. Again, a highly industrialized society makes allowing for different sleep patterns rather difficult. The average work day is about eight hours, and the work week is five or six days; most people must structure themselves and their habits within this framework. Sometimes adapting to this can cause severe sleep problems like insomnia, the inability to sleep. The fine balance of sleeping and wakefulness, which is necessary for a person's health, is difficult to achieve, and many of us take years to develop a pattern which allows us to feel our best.

It's difficult to coordinate personal cycles with societal ones. But for health to be maximized, we must do all in our power to ensure our natural cycles are as close to a personal comfort level as possible. It would be disastrous to interfere with the rise and setting of the sun, or the ebb and flow of the tides. It is just as disastrous to reorganize personal life cycles to the extent that they damage the body's health system.

These cycles can be affected by our dressing habits. Tradition has adapted us to special garments for sleeping, and most westernized countries provide some form of specialized wearing contraptions for menstruating women.* We do not really have specialized eating garments although we do often "dress for dinner," a much more social consideration than one of comfort or health.

However, dressing for dinner (or breakfast or lunch), as well as for sleep and sexual cycles is extremely important. The taking in of food is not simply a matter of choosing a food, chewing, swallowing, and digesting it. All these processes require a healthy atmosphere, both internal and external, to carry them out successfully for the greatest benefit of the body. Sleepwear, too, should be based more on comfort than on glamour. Sexually enticing nightwear should not be called sleepwear at all since its function is intended to induce activity that is quite the opposite of sleep. Anything that cuts off blood circulation or inhibits breathing is as unhealthy for sleeping as it is for eating.

When clothing is worn to allow the body to function with comfort and ease, it can flow with its individual cycles. This paves the way for the body to be healthy and happy.

Harmony and the Homeostasis of the Body

The living being is an agency of such sort that each disturbing influence induces by itself the calling forth of compensatory activity to neutralize or repair the disturbance. The higher in the scale of living beings, the more numerous, the more perfect and the more complicated do these regulatory agencies become. They tend to free the organism completely from the unfavorable influences and changes occurring in the environment.

Leon Fredericq, 1885

In his book, *The Wisdom of the Body*, Dr. Walter Cannon claimed that the body has learned to maintain itself at a constant and harmonious state. We have evolved many stabilizing (homeostatic)

---

* See Resources section for information on Seapons, the Solviva Natural Sea Silk Menstrual Sponge.

devices to counteract the effects of environment and remain alive in dangerous situations. However, external influences may affect our bodies and disrupt the natural performance of our systems. These include environmental contaminants that invade the body from the air, our food, and our clothes; medicines, which may be destructive to healthy tissue; and activities, which may disturb the balance so carefully developed over millions of years.

Because we are human, however, and possess the great gift of adaptability, we are able to aid our bodies in combating harmful environmental bombardment and to help it maintain its healthy harmonies. We can do this by eating well, exercising, and getting proper rest. Our clothing can help in achieving and maintaining equilibrium.

One of the most important aspects of this equilibrium is temperature or climate. The normal body temperature is 98.6 degrees F; in order for the body to remain healthy, it must be kept close to that temperature. The layer of air near the skin's surface is sometimes called a private climate, and skin may be looked upon as a type of clothing which protects the inner organs. However, it's important to note that skin alone is not sufficient to protect the body's private climate when the temperature of the environment drops below or above a comfortable zone.

Body temperature is held at a constant, and neither cooling nor sweating occurs at a range of environmental temperature known as the zone of vasomotor control. The surface blood vessels contract and dilate, regulating the blood (and heat) flow to the surface. When it's cold, surface vessels contract and blood flow is reduced. In hot conditions, the surface blood vessels dilate, and blood flow is increased.

If a body gets too cold and the internal temperature drops below 86 degrees F, the protective responses are reduced, respiration drops, and shivering, which is a normal, involuntary reaction that attempts to increase the metabolic rate and to raise temperature, may fail. On the other hand, if the body gets too hot, with internal temperatures of above 105.8 degrees F, the body will not be able to maintain sweat production (a cooling mechanism) and will exhaust itself in an effort to produce enough sweat to dissipate the heat. Death occurs if the body temperature drops to 77 degrees F or rises to 109.4 degrees F.

The body is subject to pain in extremes of temperature. Vasoconstriction, which occurs in cold temperatures, causes much pain. Heat stress may cause heart palpitations, accompanied by oppressive chest sensations, headache, giddiness, nausea, and a feeling of heat in the whole body.

Different cultures have suited themselves to their climates by what they wear, and we can learn much from them. There is an ancient Chinese saying: "Dress always in the color of the seasons: black in winter, white in summer, and with the color of the forests in the months in between." We might add to this: dress with the fabric of the season also — wool in winter, cotton in summer, and varying blends of these in between.

In hot climates, clothing should provide a barrier against the sun's radiation and protect the skin from reflection of heat off the surroundings. However, the clothes must not impede sweating and must not constrict the movement of air over the skin to evaporate the sweat. As clothing for this kind of environment, the woolen cloak of desert people covers the arms and legs, protects against the sun's radiation, provides insulation against the cold of night and permits water evaporation.

Many of the robes and headdresses of Middle Eastern nations offer much protection from the elements. Interestingly, in the sixteenth century, Parisian ladies who had visited these lands were so impressed with the *abbayah's* (a garment that covers the entire body) protection of their fancy dresses from mud and dirt, they tried unsuccessfully to introduce it to French fashion at home. A modern day adaptation of this garment is the poncho — a useful garment in all climates to shield against rain, wind, sun, and cold, and to use as a ground cover in the evenings.

In very cold climates, clothing should fit loosely to entrap a thick layer of air. Eskimo garments, perfectly suited for this climate, permit freedom of movement, and layered clothing adjusts for ventilation, which is just as important in the cold as it is in extreme heat.

Underwear should be made of wool, covered by a pile-lined garment, which is in turn covered by a thin, cotton, wind-resistant material. Large sleeves are best in this environment because the arms can be drawn in toward the chest for additional warmth. In areas of Northern China, people wear quilted layers and quilted eiderdown parkas that are windproofed — the perfect protection in this severe climate.

The temperate climate can be notoriously fickle as anyone who lives in this latitude would be inclined to agree. The temperature ranges from very warm to very cold and may be dry or wet, depending on the season. Changes in clothing design are appropriate for this climate. The clothing of the arctic and the desert may be modified and adapted to suit the needs for this climate by removing or adding layers, changing the fabrics, or loosening and tightening them as needed.

A healthy body also requires a nutritionally sound diet to work at its best level. As the optimum health of the body is achieved with good food, it makes all the more sense to keep it comfortable in a structurally and aesthetically sound wardrobe.

There is a parallel between eating low on the food chain and dressing low on the technology chain — eating a well-balanced diet from the earth of seeds, nuts, vegetables, and grains and wearing simply loomed, natural-fiber clothes as opposed to eating rich, fat-laden meats and heavily processed foods or wearing chemically produced, heavily processed clothes.

Proper breathing, unimpeded circulation, and good nutrition all contribute to the flow of energy in the body. Clothing that cuts off this flow by hampering the breath, the circulatory system, or the digestion of foods that have been carefully chosen to make the body healthy is disastrous to this flow of energy and in the long run is extremely detrimental to health.

Part 2

8

The natural dresser

Submit to Nature if you would reach your goal. For whoever deviates from Nature's way, Nature forces back again. Whoever gives up his desire to improve upon Nature will find Nature satisfying all his needs.

Lao Tsu, in the *Tao*

Who are "natural dressers?" Natural dressers are people who are aware of health! They are conscious of their place in society, free of the hang-ups of "shoulds" and "don'ts," people aware of their own value regardless of the values society dictates. For them, dressing is self-expressive rather than culture-expressive. Natural dressers wear what *looks,* and *feels* best for them; not what looks best to to society.

Natural dressing can be fun as people start to open their minds to what looks best. When creativity begins to flow, dressing can be a joy, not a hang-up.

Natural dressers also care about the environment; they are

concerned with pollution, the use of precious natural resources, environmental hazards, and the economic ramifications of these problems. Natural dressers are healthy consumers: they use only what they need, dressing so the mind, body, and spirit coalesce. If one lives in harmony with the self, one lives in harmony with the universe.

Blueprints for the Natural Dresser's Wardrobe

The body is a remarkable system that takes measures to protect itself, rejuvenate itself, and preserve itself in equilibrium with the universe. But there are conditions under which the system can not maintain itself without aid from our consciousness and external efforts. Indeed there are conditions which we impose on our bodies that may cause it harm: poor diets, lack of exercise, environmental hazards, and poor clothing.

In an effort to alleviate some of these hazards — the dressing aspect — we have devised some suggestions and ideas for a natural dresser. This is, of course, a new area to explore. As pioneers, we do not yet know all the answers but our awareness is increasing. These new avenues of exploration in finding healthier ways to dress make for an exciting journey toward developing the types of clothes that enhance, envelop, protect, and preserve our bodies.

Until now too much attention has been paid to the effect clothes have on the beholder, rather than their effects on the wearer. The idea of looking good seems to mean a finished package that is presented to the world: clothes neatly polished, cinched, ironed — each part of the body sectioned, isolated from the other. Even the words used to describe dressing make our bodies sound like pieces of metal to be manipulated and honed to perfection.

As far as clothes are concerned, the body is certainly not viewed holistically. Each part receives its own cover to separate it from the next. No attention is paid to the flow of energy through nerve paths. We've been so concerned with efficiency in our work clothes and frivolity in our clothes worn for leisure that the actual concern for our bodies has been nonexistent.

More recently some high-fashion designers have attempted to introduce "body conscious" clothes to the market. Although many of these types of clothes are more flowing and conform a bit more with the shape of the body, the emphasis is placed on exhibiting and emphasizing parts of the body — the breasts, legs, or buttocks — for sexual allure. This type of emphasis is not a healthy attitude about the body and in many ways preserves and promulgates unhealthy sexual stereotyping, something which is certainly not new to fashion. Body consciousness should not mean that the body is exposed or its parts voyeuristically overemphasized, rather it should mean a consciousness of how well the clothing fits the body, not how well the body fits the clothes.

The human body has evolved to walk upright, work, and play in its environment and to adapt to extremes in climate; our clothing can be designed to facilitate this evolution. We can also learn many things from history and other cultures about dressing and incorporate some of these ideas for the wardrobe of the natural dresser.

In chapter 5 we discussed the structure of the body and showed that it was a marvelous piece of architecture and not just a hanger for clothes. Utilizing our knowledge of the way the body is put together, we can develop designs for clothing that work with the natural lines and points of support of the body.

There are two major points of support that form the major support structure for the body: the shoulder girdle and the pelvic girdle. As the skin is draped over the muscles and skeletal structure, so too may clothes be draped with their basic support stemming from the shoulder or the pelvis.

Dressing along the points of support frees body lines, does not inhibit organs or muscles, helps retain body heat and moisture, and does not isolate limbs. The body is draped rather than trussed up and restricted. There are other skeletal points of support that are more changeable than the shoulder or pelvis. Elbows, when bent, support fabric, as do knees, and when they are straightened, the material again flows freely.

Secondary support is provided by the fleshy parts of the body, particularly the abdomen and the buttocks. These are areas that rise and contract, or undulate in some way upon some movement in the body (breathing, digestion, to name a few). More often than not, these secondary points of support are severely restricted and squeezed in by belts, corsets, and tight clothing.

Dressing with the points of support in mind has many beneficial aspects: respiratory, circulatory, and homeostatic systems can function healthily, and nerve energy can flow freely. Muscles can

Fig. 8–1. The simple geometric shapes of mantles allow for free body movement.

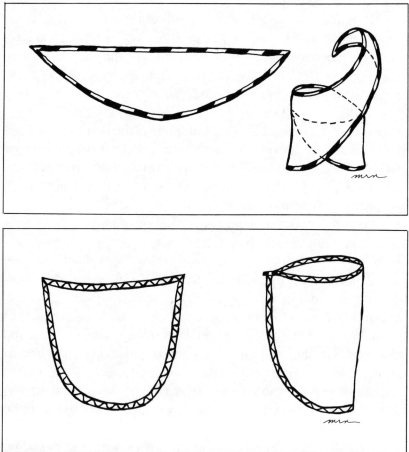

expand and contract readily, and the body is not forced into unnatural or uncomfortable postures. Because the lines of the body aren't interrupted or cross-sectioned by binding belts or tight, restrictive clothes, garments can be layered for warmth and regulated to periodic bodily size changes either as a result of weight or style change. Since it is draped, the body retains its basic thermostatic control. The body can function as a whole, not with highly specialized parts that are separate from each other. Dressing this way permits clothes to

become expressions of the self and the body, not the society and its restrictions.

Using these support concepts as a base, one can begin designing a natural wardrobe incorporating the basic clothing shapes worn by people in ancient civilizations. Among the early Greeks, Egyptians, and Etruscans, the body was esteemed as a holy object to be adorned and treated with the utmost respect. The artistic principle of draping the figure to idealize its form was applied to clothing the body, and this idea is valuable to natural dressing today.

One of the earliest form of dress incorporated simple geometric shapes to create what is known as a mantle. Mantles are ovals made of heavy woolen fabric. It cloaks the body to allow free arm movement, the neck is left free, and the breathing anatomy is not obstructed. Mantles also allow for layering underneath.

A round version of the mantle is called the *tebenna*. This is an elegant shape that has characteristics similar to the oval mantle. Both these types of mantles may be made from various fabrics, and the design may be used for outer garments to provide excellent coverage against weather elements. They may be fastened over the shoulder by buttons or hooks and eyes.

Another idea for outer wear is the himation, a long rectangle of cloth that is draped over the shoulder and wound around the body. The form of the body provides a perfect framework for elegant lines with this garment.

To complement these garments, the lowly scarf — a simple geometric shape either rectangular or square — may be used as a cover for the head or the face (against wind, dust, sun, and cold). It can also be wrapped around the shoulders for added warmth. It may even be converted to a sash, which may be used to anchor other garments at the waist. The softness of natural fabrics permits a draping around the pelvic girdle, rather than cinching the waist too tightly and obstructing movement.

Mantles may take other shapes as well, triangular or rectangular. Because of their basic geometric forms and the types of fabrics used (such as soft, woven, natural fibers), these too conform readily to the contours of the body. The rectangular mantle may be draped in many ways, forming entirely different garments.

Round cloths may be folded in half to form an oval, or a hole may be cut in the center for the head to form a simple poncho. Squares of fabrics may be folded diagonally to form a triangular mantle (similar to a shawl). Any of these may be fastened by buttons, toggles, pins, or sashes made with other shapes.

9

Texture

The elements of design are built into clothes by the nature of the fabric — its texture, fiber, and color. Design is also influenced by line and form. Line serves to outline, connect, and contour shape. The eye travels along the path of a line, whether straight or curved, zigzag or diagonal, vertical or horizontal.

Line has one dimension: length. Form adds the other dimensions — volume and space — that make up the whole image. Clothing can complement the form of the body by flowing with its lines; it can camouflage the body by covering the form of the body, and it can restrict and hamper the body by forcing the form into unnatural, ungraceful, and uncomfortable lines.

Textures add the properties of size, bulk, shape, light, and weight to fabrics. Common characteristics of fabrics, softness or roughness, for example, should be considered when different fabrics are worn together. Fashion experts agree that with careful selection textures may produce physical illusions that are beneficial to the appearance of the individual. Contrast in texture, as in color, emphasizes form. Thus a small person may get lost in a fabric with a large-patterned texture, and large and heavy people will appear bigger in this type of garment.

Stiff-textured clothes stand away from the body and hide any irregularities. However, if the fabric is too stiff, the body may appear bulkier and heavier. This is neither good for very thin people, who may be dwarfed by the contrast, nor for heavier people, who may appear thicker. Bulky knits also add weight and thickness and should be considered when deciding how much space one wishes to create the illusion of occupying.

Clingy and soft fabrics are comfortable and show the natural form of the body. This is desirable for a healthy, well-toned individual. Shiny clothes make people appear larger, as do heavy-pile weaves such as velvets and velours. On the other hand, dull-textured fabrics absorb light and do not add bulk to the body.

Feeling with Eyes

The appearance of a surface is our first experience of how the substance will feel. What we see is a direct result of the reflection or absorption of light. As light reflects off the surface of a piece of cloth, it is translated by our eyes into something that will be understood by our skin via the sensation of touch. The texture of a heavily woven garment can be anticipated because of sight; so too can that of a sheer, silk scarf. Messages transmitted by the visual image are quickly interpreted, and we can easily decide whether or not we'd like the feel of the article on our skin or not. This is an important discrimination factor in choosing healthy clothes: if we like the way something looks, chances are we'll be positively predisposed to what it will feel like.

Children are extremely perceptive in assessing texture with their eyes. They might readily claim that something looks "yucky" and absolutely refuse to touch it. Their little bodies are extremely sensitive to external stimuli; because they have not become jaded and hardened, they can respond healthily, often gutsily, to these sensations. Healthy adult dressers should be encouraged to trust the visual judgements they have about things they wear. If a garment's texture does not look right to them or looks uncomfortable, chances are it will be just that. Conversely, clothing that looks soft and comfortable will probably feel that way too. Each of us who has seen the sheen and luster of a fine silk shirt instinctively knows the fabric will be comfortable.

Texture may also be used as a statement to present a healthy and happy image to the world. Cotton pique, lightweight wool jerseys, and dull linens are fine for people who wish to remain fairly inconspicuous. But if one wishes to create a more dramatic and vibrant relationship with the world, texture experimentation can play an important role as people learn how their sense of touch energizes them and those around them.

The final judgement about whether or not a garment will be comfortable must, of course, be made when it's put on the body. But all our senses can help in decision-making processes and a holistic approach to healthy dressing encourges all aspects.

Raw Materials

The raw materials of the fabric — the fibers, yarns, weaves, as well as the finishes put on them — determine the feel or hand of a cloth — its coarseness, rigidity, crispness, or softness. Fibers are the fine, hairlike substances which are spun into yarns and woven into cloth. These fibers may be natural in origin — such as wool, cotton, linen, and silk — or man-made — such as polyesters and acrylics. Short fibers, like cotton, produce dull finishes; long filaments, like silk, produce shiny ones.

The texture of yarn is determined in part by the manner in which the fibers are twisted and spun. A yarn with a low number of twists will be shiny, while one with a higher twist will be rough. Yarns can be twisted so they'll stretch easily, or they can be prepared to produce a fuzzy texture when they're brushed. Also determining texture is the way the fabric is put together. This can be done by knitting, weaving, felting, and braiding.

Texture is produced in weaving by using warp and filling yarns of different diameters; also, one dimension may be made closer together than the other. Closely woven fabrics keep their shape better and shrink less; loosely woven ones are more porous and lightweight, but in choosing them one must be careful the fabric is not cheaply made because it may not be durable to give good wear.

Many durable fabrics and those with the softest feel are made with a plain weave. These include cotton weaves of percale, gingham, chambray, lawn, flannelette, dress and handkerchief linen; silk shirting, chiffon, and crepe de chine; as well as homespun wools, challis, crepe, and soft tweed. The plain-weave method may also be used for some blends of these fibers. These fabrics may not have the most interesting textures, but they are comfortable to wear.

Twill weaves, in which yarns are woven to form diagonal ridges called wales, are the most durable. Because of their durability, twill weaves are usually used for men's suiting. They show dirt less but are harder to clean than plain-woven cloths. Among the fabrics made with twill weave are cotton jeans, denims, gabardine, khaki, serge, silk serge, and surah cloth. Wool tweed and worsted, which are long-staple wool fibers, are also twill weaves that are combed for softness.

A third type of simple weave is the satin, or sateen, weave. This reflects light better than twill or plain weaves. Silks and cottons may be made with satin weaves. Because of their characteristic shine and light reflections, they add bulk to the wearer. They are also very expensive to produce.

Fancy weaves, such as pile, Jacquard, dobby, and leno, are the ones that have the kinds of texture most perceptible to the eye and hand. Pile weaves create soft and downy textures like velvets and velours. Absorbent terry-cloth garments and durable corduroys are also made with this weave.

Jacquards are extremely complicated fabrics made on intricate looms. These have the most interesting textures of all and are basically used for brocades in clothing. Dobby weaves are small designs woven into fabrics and are used primarily in diapers, cotton madras shirts, and in some men's suitings. Leno weaves, which make open-weave cloths, are usually not used for natural-fiber clothes.

Texture is also made by knitting fibers together. Knitting, as weaving, may be done by hand or by a machine, and a number of stitches make up the range of creative, texturized fabrics. The size and texture of the yarns, as well as the size of the needles used in knitting, will determine the texture of the fabric. All of the stitches used for knitting may be combined to form interesting textures and designs for wearing apparel. The weave or knit of a fabric can make a difference in both the comfort and the look of the clothes worn. Although machines can do stitches faster than by hand, hand-knitted and woven fabrics are more interesting to look at and have a more natural feel; plus they offer the added pleasure of being made with human energy, touch, and feelings. These aspects impart added value to healthy clothing and make dressing a component of healthy living.

Although the feel of cloth is produced by the type of fiber used and the design in which it is fashioned, the most important aspect of a cloth's feel is its texture. The weave of a garment will determine the type of stimulation our skin receives, making us feel well or not. Texture is extremely important to the natural dresser and much experimentation should go into determining the best texture of the clothing worn. The texture that makes a person happiest, carefully coupled with healthy color and extended by body-loving designs, make our clothes second skins truly worth wearing.

10

Color

Using color in healing and therapy is as old as recorded history. Every culture has in some way incorporated the use of special hues to encourage well-being and bodily protection and, in some instances, to conjure evil spirits and ill health against enemies. While much of this color medicine is viewed by modern people as primitive and magic and sorcery, the result of ignorance and superstition, the ancients regarded color as divine and in no way treated its use lightly. Red was used to encourage health; blue, for virtue and faith; yellow, for happiness and prosperity; green, for fertility; and white for protection from heaven.

Color, in the form of precious or semiprecious stones has been worn for healing. Brown agate aided fevers and epilepsy; amber was used to relieve stomach aches. Green beryl and emeralds relieved eye diseases, and yellow beryl cured jaundice. Jade was used to help childbirth, while lapis lazuli (a blue stone) prevented miscarriage. Sapphires were believed to prevent the plague.

Red, the most significant color in the healing spectrum was thought to prevent and cure anything from hemorrhaging to smallpox. In England, physicians wore red cloaks to distinguish themselves as healers and wrapped patients in scarlet blankets to alleviate their ills. Red wool has been worn to cure sprains, sore throats, and fevers. Black, too, was seen as an effective color. Black animal skins were believed to relieve rheumatism.

Though not necessarily health related, the Aztecs used colored robes and garments during sacrificial ceremonies both for priests and victims because the colors were seen as good "medicine" to appease the gods. Native Americans felt color was extremely important to health and created color wheels that related colors to seasons, animals, temperament, and health care.

What role does color play in modern dressing? Colors have fashion cycles just as hemlines and tie widths have, and this forms the basis of many choices clothing consumers make. The hot, fluorescent pinks and oranges of the sixties quickly became passé for the fashion-conscious of the seventies. Colors also impart social messages about the wearers: investment bankers must wear somber colors, modern day healers wear white, and only children are free to wear all the colors of the rainbow.

But, the main point of dressing for health is to choose clothing that makes the wearers feel good — and this will make them look good, too. The ancients believed that color affects the way we feel, and so do we. Indeed, there is a modern science, called chromopathy, which is attempting to document the ways that color affects people. Knowing about both the psychological and physical properties of color, we can use color as a powerful design element in our wardrobes.

The first recorded experiments on light were done in the seventeenth century by Sir Isaac Newton, who discovered that light passed through a prism bends into a spectrum of colors. He proved that color does not exist in the absence of light and named the seven hues in the spectrum: red, orange, yellow, green, blue, indigo, and violet. Because each color radiates from the sun at a different energy rate (wavelength) the order of these colors is fixed. Red has the longest wavelength, violet the shortest.

All color systems, the way colors are described and defined, are based on this spectrum. The spectrum band can be twisted to form a circle — the color wheel. For purposes of dress, the Prang color system is most useful. This is based on three primary colors that are placed equidistant from each other on the color wheel; the color produced midway between two neighboring primaries is called a secondary color, and an intermediate hue is created by a combination of a primary and neighboring secondary hue.

The color black is viewed as the absence of light. When it is mixed with other colors, it changes their appearance, and modifies our perception of the color. For example, black added to orange will produce brown. On the other hand, the color white is seen as light itself. Both black and white are the producers of value for color and provide the nuances of tints and shades in the spectrum.

Designing with Color

Colors are sometimes divided into primary or secondary systems, but for natural dressing and health, the dimensions of color — hue, value, and intensity of each one we wear — are more important.

Hue relates to nature; it is the property of color that makes it appear warm or cool. A warm hue is that of fire or the sun: red, orange, and yellow. Cool hues are of the sky and water: blue, green, and violet. Hues carry the illusion of weight: red, orange, and yellow are called advancing hues because they make an object appear to be moving forward. These colors emphasize the body's size and shape and make things appear larger. Blues, greens, and violets are receding hues and make objects appear smaller, farther away and minimize their size and shape.

Understanding color hues is important in natural dressing because it helps to create a personal and psychological sense of well-being. If a person is agitated, wearing a cooler hue may produce a calming effect; on the other hand, wearing a warm color may make a depressed person feel gayer and happier.

Value refers to the lightness or darkness of a color. If white is added to red, pink is produced, which has a higher value than red. This is called a tint. Conversely, if black is added to red, the color will have a lower value, be darker. This is called a shade. If gray is added, the color is toned. Chroma refers to the purity or intensity of a color. It is expressed in a color's brightness or dullness or in its strength or weakness. Colors with high chroma are brilliant and strong; those with low chroma are dull and weak.

What does all of this technical information have to do with healthy dressing? Tints, shades, tones, and chroma add drama to clothing as well as camouflage to the body. These are important psychological factors and add a sense of individuality to our manner of dressing. Values relate to hues in that extremes of lightness or darkness will emphasize the body's appearance. Values allow for contrast with the environment. This is important because the eye is attracted to an area where there is sharp contrast, which in turn emphasizes the area. A person who wishes to camouflage an area of the body should avoid wearing contrast in that body area. Contrasting designs and color are often built into the clothes we wear by belts, trims, and patterns. A proper understanding of the values of color can help a person dress more comfortably to express individuality rather than conformity. Chroma adds personality and flair to chosen clothing. A high-chroma color can direct attention to an area of the body one wishes to emphasize. High-chroma colors, like light hues, make the body appear larger.

Clothes with high-chroma colors can make hair and eye color less intense. They also force or emphasize complementary colors. For example, a bright green dress can make a person with a ruddy complexion look crimson, or a violet garment may make a person look jaundiced by bringing out the yellowness in a sallow complexion. High chroma, however, need not be detrimental to a person's looks. On the contrary, an intense color may complement a person's body coloring. An orange scarf, for example, will emphasize blue eyes. The chart below provides some guidelines for designing with color in mind:

Hue	Value	Chroma	Effect
red, orange, yellow	light tints, strong contrasts	strong, high intensity	increases body-size appearance
blue, green, purple	low tones, weak contrasts	weak, low intensity	decreases body-size appearance

Color Coordination and Harmonies

Seeing color is a psychological experience, and color preferences are based on a number of social, cultural, and emotional aspects. There are, however, factors that make some color combinations more pleasing than others because some colors are related while others are contrasted. Related colors share one hue in common; contrasting ones have none in common. For example, yellow is related to orange because it helps to make the color, and blue is related to green because it is a component of the color. On the other hand, blue and yellow are contrasting hues because they have no hue in common.

All living things are related and live at their healthiest best when they are in harmony with the world. Color is one of the best ways individuals can adjust themselves to living harmoniously with their environments. The innate qualities of color and their adaptabilities to each other offer us a palette with which we can paint our lives. Artists and color theorists have devised ways for arranging palettes that can be helpful for us in designing one for ourselves.

Harmonizing colors is one way of creating a palette. There are two kinds of harmonies for related colors: monochromatic, which uses the same hue for tints, tones, and shades; and analogous, which uses colors that lie next to each other in the color wheel. Chromatic harmonies may appear monotonous if the value and intensity of the colors are too close. They may also look mismatched for this reason. Experimenting with monochromatic harmonies is an exercise in developing a sense of subtlety. Effectively combining hues in this manner can create a serene personal environment of clothing that is pleasant for both the wearer and the people who are near.

Analogous harmonies can be striking and dramatic because they create visual vibrations. If the lightness or darkness, as well as the purity of the colors, are varied, a personal statement that spells vibrant good health and happiness may be expressed.

There is a system for contrasting colors as well, called complementary harmonies, colors that are opposite each other on the color wheel. Red with green and blue-violet with yellow-orange are examples of complementary harmonies. If complementary colors are used in their highest intensity, the combination may be too vivid. This is easily remedied by wearing a complementary hue in a smaller area or by toning or shading the hue. Complementary hues affect body coloring also. Red skin will appear redder and pink skin, pinker, if green is worn next to it. Yellow skin will appear more sallow if violet or red/blue-violet are worn next to it. Again, experimentation is needed to see which complements in what intensity work best for the individual.

Healthy dressing can be enhanced by using both related and contrasting color harmonies that express inner feelings. Bodies can become palettes for painting a creative, healthy, and beautiful image enjoyed by us and others around us.

Spiritual Aspects of Color

Astrologers have long expressed the importance of color to individuals born under the zodiac signs, and color theorists concur that colors are related to the planets. In fact colors and planets often share properties. The following chart was condensed from the "Cycles of Experience" chart from *The Rainbow Book, A Collection of Essays and Illustrations Devoted to Rainbows in Particular and Spectral Sequences in General,* edited by F. Lanier Graham (© The Fine Arts Museum of San Francisco, Vintage Books, 1979).

We can see from the chart there is literally a wide spectrum of colors from which one can choose a wardrobe that encompasses spiritual and physical well-being. The fact that red may be associated with Aries or Scorpio and green with Sagittarius, need not mean that only those born under those planetary influences should wear these colors. On the contrary, knowing the properties of the colors and the properties of the related planets can help people to determine the qualities they would like to make a part of their lives, to include the colors that may work best for their lifestyles and health, and to eliminate those whose energy is not charged enough or is too powerful for their ideal. For example, green is associated with healing, and the related planet Jupiter numbers optimism among its properties. People wishing to encourage these qualities may wish to

Color	Properties of Color	Related Planet	Properties of Planet	Zodiac Sign Ruled
Red	Birth, Beginning, Heat, Heart, Primal matter, Violent change	Mars	Passion, Desire, Energy, Initiative, Violent change, War	Aries Scorpio
Orange	Power, Glory, Radiant energy, Sun, Kiss of life	Sun Venus	Life, Vitality, Illumination, Will, Leadership	Leo
Yellow	Intellect, Joy, Sensation, Brightness	Mercury	Intelligence, Logic, Mental activity, Communication, Speed	Gemini Virgo
Green	Growth, Youth, Healing, Vegetation	Jupiter	Enthusiasm, Good fortune, Optimism, Spontaneity	Sagittarius Pisces
Blue	Spirit, Sky, Heaven, Prayer, Psychic	Saturn	Limitation, Caution, Crystallization, Time	Aquarius Capricorn
Indigo	Intuition, Seeking, Sorrow, Beauty, Spirituality	Uranus Venus	Beauty, Harmony, Love, the Arts	Libra Taurus
Violet	Transition, Death, Separation, Yearning, Advanced spirituality	Moon	Instinct, Feeling, Subconscious, Receptivity	Cancer

choose a green palette for their wardrobes, perhaps using mono-chromatic harmonies ranging from the palest lime to the deepest jade and contrasting the clothing with complementary hues, a pale pink shawl or deep rose sash. These tints and shades of red can add just the right amount of energy and warmth needed to make the wearer feel complete.

Orange is the color of the "kiss of life." This color could do much to enhance a person's well-being. One can imagine the effects of wearing a soft cotton caftan that envelopes the body in its radiant energy, instilling in the wearer life and vitality. It could not help but make a person feel well and happy and to generate an aura of health.

Yellow is thought to affect metabolism and also has the practical aspect of being a good color for safety because it reflects light well. Yellow clothing is good for outdoor nightwear, particularly for joggers and cyclists. Greens are suggested for meditative activities. Blue is also restful. Interestingly, blue is known as the world's favorite color.

Just as the color of our surrounding is important to how we feel, so too are the colors of our clothes. Our clothes are like individual environments we take wherever we go. If we're comfortable in them, and if the colors suit both our moods and activities, chances are we will not only feel better about the things we have to do, we will actually be healthier!

11

The basics for the wardrobe

The basic blueprints for the natural dresser's wardrobe were borrowed from the clothing ideas of the Etruscans and the early Greeks and Romans. Making a geographic and historic move, we can also use some of the ideas of the Middle East.

The garments worn in desert countries utilize a concept of housing the body. These clothes retain body moisture, which cools it in the heat of the day, and the clothes retain heat for the cool evenings. They allow the body to move as a whole unit, rather than in segmented parts. They also lend themselves to centering the body and are useful for meditation.

Among these types of clothes are caftans, which are worn by Arabs, Turks, and Egyptians. Another type of desert garment is the burnoose worn by the Arabs and Moors. This is a sleeveless woolen cloak with a hood. Still another is the *djarellaba* from Morocco, a full, loose, hooded garment made in varying lengths from wool or cotton. Another Middle Eastern garment, the *abbayah* is a woolen or cotton cloak that covers the entire body. It is worn as protection from heat and dust and also affords the wearer a sense of privacy. All of these garments are most adaptable to modern living because of their simplicity and ease of line. They can be worn either short or long and may be adorned with designs and embroidery. They can also be worn with other articles of clothing.

Needless to say, the wardrobe for the natural dresser is eclectic; in borrowing ideas from other cultures, we should not overlook the additions that the yogis have given us. These are clothes that do not bind or chafe and that allow tremendous flexibility of movement to the body. They include drawstring pants, which allow the easy loosening of the garment during physical exercise and provide breathing room by not cinching the waist with a hard belt.

Drawstring pants may be fashioned from cotton, corduroy, silk, and wool to suit the climate. The legs are roomy and may also be fashioned with drawstrings at the ankle. A related garment called Berber trousers are loose-flowing pants with a drawstring waist and strings at the ankle to give the pants a bloused shape. This can provide a warming or cooling effect depending upon the fabric used.

Harem pants are similar to Berber trousers. Although the name may not be attractive, the pants are; they provide comfort and freedom of movement for women. These, too, are bloused at the ankle by drawstrings and may be made in silk, cotton, or wool. They offer the freedom of pants with the flowing coverage of a long skirt. The traditional upper garment for yoga is called a *kurta.* It may be made from cotton, silk, or wool. The simple cut allows for freedom of movement through the shoulders and arms, and the loose tunic style provides breathing room as well as a becoming drape for the body. An obi (sash), can accompany the *kurta* for a dressier look.

Kurtas normally have bell-type sleeves with enough width in the armhole and wrist to permit the freest movement possible. These may be layered over cotton undershirts for added warmth. Drawstring pants and *kurtas* may be worn by men and women. Because they are loose, consideration may be given to the anatomical differences between the sexes. The drawstring waist usually falls a bit below the waist, and the support of the garment rests on the hips (pelvic girdle). *Kurtas* may be designed with buttons on the sleeve

Fig. 11–1. *A loose-fitting cotton sweatshirt worn under a sweater wears well with soft, brushed-denim dungarees with a wrap waist. Leather moccasins complete the look.* (Drawing by Curt Wagner)

Fig. 11–2. *Cocoon caftan worn over cotton t-shirt and soft cotton wrap skirt. Heavier fabrics can be used for cooler weather.* (Photos for this chapter by Mats Nordström) (Outfit courtesy of Three Wishes, New York)

and loops at the end, so they can be rolled up and kept out of the way during work. Another shirt that can be worn by either men or women is a simple cotton sweatshirt which can be layered over t-shirts and under sweaters.

Returning to clothes that are worn in the West, there are several designs and styles that may be adopted by the natural dresser. The drawstring skirt has the same waistband as the pants. This can be loosened or tightened to adjust to the normal fluctuations of the abdomen and waist. These skirts may be fashioned from all the natural fibers; decorated with designs, embroidery, appliqués; and made in different lengths from knee to foot.

Wrap-around skirts also adapt to the shape of the body and allow for natural movements. These, too, may be made in varying lengths, fabrics, and designs. They may be fastened by buttons, ties, or hooks and eyes. It should be noted that both drawstring and wrap skirts may be designed with a slight or wide flare, or with a fairly straight shape worn close to the body. In figure 11–2, our model is wearing a cotton wrap skirt with a sleeveless cotton t-shirt and a cotton cocoon caftan. All the garments flow easily with the body and are very comfortable for warm days.

The kilt is a garment worn in ancient times by both the Sumerians and the Egyptians and more recently by the Scots. It is usually made from wool, patterned in plaids, and comes to a length just about to the knee. The kilt is similar in design to a wrap skirt and has an additional fastener which clasps the fabric together at mid-thigh.

Shorts may be worn by men or women. These, too, should have a drawstring waist. They should not bind in any way around the upper knee or thigh. Shorts may be made in a variety of fabrics. They are particularly useful for leisure wear in warm climates. Overalls or coveralls are usually associated with painters, plumbers, and electricians. These garments allow for free movement and also protect anything worn underneath from paint and dirt. One of the most important aspects of this garment is the point of support it employs — the shoulder. Overalls are usually fastened at each shoulder and are fairly loose over the body, particularly at the waist/diaphragm/abdomen level. They need not only be worn for work, however;

they may be made from many different fabrics — everything from silk to cotton canvas. They lend themselves to layering for warmth. This type of garment in a light fabric is recommended for summer weather because of the absence of constriction to the body, it's dependence on the shoulder for support (rather than the waist), and the bellows action permitting freedom of movement to the body.

Another type garment for warm weather consists of two pieces: a loose upper jacket with long sleeves (that roll up) and buttons and shorts that have a loose waistband. The shorts should be fastened by straps which pass over the shoulder, or the jacket could be fastened to the shorts with toggles.

Fig. 11–3. *Lightweight shorts are ideal for summer weather. She has on cotton drawstring shorts with a cotton tube top and pima cotton overshirt. He is wearing a silk shirt and drawstring pants.* (Outfits courtesy of Three Wishes, New York)

Fig. 11–4. *Guatemalan poncho.* (Courtesy of Putumayo, New York)

Fig. 11–5. *Down-filled coat.* (Courtesy of Tamala Design with Bagel, New York)

One of the most versatile garments in any climate is the poncho. The one shown in the photograph (fig. 11–4) is heavy Guatemalan cotton, but ponchos can be made from wool or any other natural fiber. They are warm and can protect the body from snow or rain. They can also be used as a ground cover.

Perhaps one of the best ways to insure warmth in clothing is through quilting, which sandwiches other materials between outer layers. The coat shown in figure 11–5 is a cotton shell filled with down. This is one of the warmest coats available and can be made in a shorter, jacket version.

Animal hair and wool fibers make very warm garments. The coat in figure 11–6 is camel hair. It is surprisingly soft — and the drape of this design is at once elegant and functional. The large collar protects the neck and head, and the sleeves are full enough to

Fig. 11–6. *Flowing camel hair coat.* (Courtesy of Three Wishes, New York)

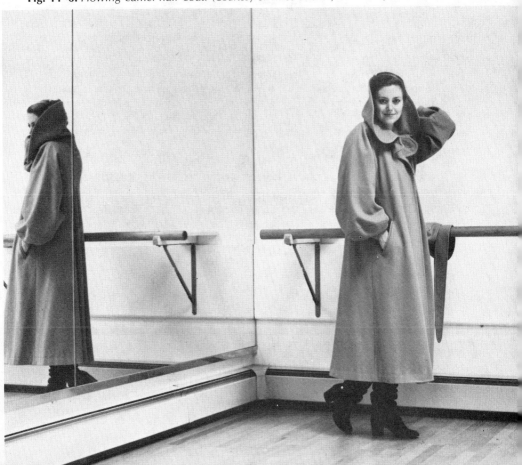

Fig. 11–7. *She is wearing the same camel coat as in the previous picture; this time she wears it belted. He is wearing a reversible mohair and wool coat that is very warm and does not restrict movement.* (Courtesy of Three Wishes, New York)

allow a sweater to be layered underneath without restricting movement. The same coat is belted in figure 11–7, but still retains its comfortable look and flowing lines.

12

Little dressing

Life is reasserted, replenished, re-established through the birth of every new generation — our children. They are the future, the inheritors of culture, society, environment, and lifestyles.

When it comes to children almost everyone agrees that we should do the best for them in all ways. The means of going about this may differ, but generally there is agreement that children need and deserve a good, solid base on which to grow and blossom. Children who have been given a sound, nurturing beginning — nutritionally, psychologically, and physically — usually thrive very well in life, even during times of stress or illness. Providing the healthiest environment possible is essential.

Because children are very adaptable, they learn in their early life all that is shown to them. Habits formed early in life remain throughout their lives, and good dressing habits can do much in aiding the inheritors of the planet to learn to live harmoniously with their world. In fact dramatic changes can be most easily affected through our children who are so eager to learn and to live well.

Skin, the universal covering of our bodies, is an organ of

sublime sensation capable of experiencing the gamut from pleasure to pain. The human embryo is aware of the sense of touch in the womb; if it is touched gently by an object, it will bend away from the source. Since skin is the first organ to develop, it is the one that offers us our first experiences: the ways in which we learn about our world.

All healthy living creatures respond to touch. Blindness and deafness do not prevent a person from experiencing the world; but a person who cannot feel, whether physically or emotionally, remains out of the environment and unable to communicate with surroundings. In studies done with animals, it was found that those who were not permitted the natural licking and grooming processes from their mothers became ill, were unable to grow normally or to stand, and some eventually died.

Ashley Montagu claims that "loss of touch with the body results in loss of touch with reality." Since the sense of touch is so very important to the body, it would seem that creating a reality that is gentling to the system, rather than one that is harsh or coarse in a physical sense, would be important. We respond to the way others touch us. A push, shove, or slap is met with immediate tension or a turning away from its source; a gentle stroke, soft pat on the head or back, or an embrace is met with a release of tension in the body and a feeling of security and comfort. If our clothes stimulate us in pleasant ways, our bodies can interrelate harmoniously with the environment; if they make us feel uptight, itchy, restricted, rough, too large or too small, our awareness of our place in the world will be distorted, strange, and unhappy.

To help children to develop as healthy adults it's essential that their clothing give them freedom to explore and learn and comfort their sensitive, developing bodies. Trussed up, they'll learn rigidity; covered in scratchy, harsh clothes they'll learn to be irritable. However, designing a wardrobe around security, warmth, softness, and comfort can provide a base for them to grow soundly and to reach maturity with healthful ideals they'll want to continue using for the rest of their lives.

The principles for natural dressing for children are the same as those for adults. There should be no restrictions for breathing or inhibition of movement, and it's even more important for children's clothes to be made from breathable natural fibers. It is also essential that harmful chemicals and dyes be eliminated from kids' wardrobes since their delicate skins absorb these toxins readily. Children's circulatory systems must not in any way be hampered and clothes should be loose around around their abdomen and diaphragm areas to allow for proper digestion.

Children are not miniature adults who are dressed up to mimic the so-called roles of men and women. Both boys and girls should be encouraged to use their bodies athletically; physical fitness helps children to develop holistically in body, mind, and spirit; clothes should not hamper this development. In fact, proper dress can encourage healthy play and physical growth and improvement. What must be remembered is that kids are constantly growing and strengthening themselves. Each child does this at a different pace, some faster or slower than others. There are certain age standardizations, of course, but each child is an individual. Their muscles must be permitted to develop naturally. Their bodies should be strengthened and supported; clothes should not bind the developing bodily structures.

Children go through many developmental stages in their lives, each one as important as the next. Our primary concern in this book is to present information that can help them physically. This in the long run can affect their emotional and psychological growth in a positive way.

Development begins before birth when the child is protected in its mother's womb. It is here that the basic information about physical reality — the touch and feel — is encountered. As the child is born it is initiated into the real world through more intense feelings, changeable ones, sometimes painful ones, but it's little body takes it all in to categorize and establish a relationship with its surroundings.

For the first weeks, a newborn mostly sleeps, waking occasionally to take nourishment; but basically it lives in a kind of dreamlike state with barely enough physical equipment developed to differentiate itself from its surroundings. But it feels everything from the

Fig. 12–1. *Two thoughtful boys are comfortably clad in cotton t-shirts. The boy on the left wears an appliquéd, cotton canvas overall with a striped shirt, and the boy on the right wears a string-tied cotton vest with short pants. His moccasins are very comfortable worn with cotton knee socks.* (Drawings for this chapter by Pauletta Brooks)

caress of its mother's hand to the softness of its blankets, diapers, and undershirts. It is imperative that the clothes that come into contact with the newborn's skin be of the finest quality, free from poisonous dyes, flame retardants, and other finishing chemicals.

White cottons and linens are the best fabrics for a baby's skin, and soft wools are recommended for covers, sweaters, sleepers, and kimonos. Since wool is inherently flame retardant as well as comfortable, it is the best fiber for infants' clothing.

Many newer clothes are made from synthetics that have been brushed to simulate natural cloths. However, they can never offer the comfort and breathability of natural fibers, and because many contain harmful dyes and chemicals they should not be put on an infant's body. Cotton diapers allow the baby's skin to breathe. Since they are the baby's first outside stimulus they should be loose and nonbinding and free from dyes and caustic soaps.

After a few weeks the baby begins to move about. It's important not to inhibit the infant's movement because movement is essential to the child's physical and mental development. Dresses are good garments for both sexes at this time because they do not inhibit movement, but they do cover the child adequately. Cultures that require their children to be repressed to fit in with carefully ordered societal mores take great pains to restrict their children's movement in clothes. Babies are swaddled in some cultures, virtually tied up and made unable to move as a training technique to instruct the children in acceptable patterns of behavior. Some tribal peoples believe inhibiting and frustrating angry infants' movements will eventually make them strong. In western cultures, however, allowing the child to move freely is seen to enhance healthy development.

The three most important considerations for a child's development at this stage are warmth, comfort, and cleanliness; clothes should contribute to each, and often the least amount of clothes are the best. Simple blankets wrapped loosely around the child provide for all three considerations and allow for healthy movement as well.

As the baby begins to grow, clothing requirements grow as

well. Diapers are necessary from birth, and we recommend that cotton cloths be used rather than the plastic-covered cellulose ones worn so often. In the past couple of years, we've observed a return to using cloth diapers and diaper services which provide clean (sterilized) white cotton cloths that are no more expensive than the packaged disposable diapers, which often irritate a baby's skin. Some children are allergic to the plastics in their diapers as well as the deodorants applied to them. Although plastic-covered diapers keep some moisture from contacting the skin, the wetness that remains provides a breeding ground for germs that cause diaper rash and other dermatological problems. Plastic doesn't breathe, and it's essential to put breathing fibers near an infant's body.

There is some controversy over putting shoes on infants' feet. Babies need no special support for their development, especially in their feet. On the contrary, shoes worn too early, improperly fitted, can cause severe problems for developing feet. If a foot covering for a very young infant is absolutely necessary (perhaps for warmth), it would be best to use loose-fitting booties or shoes that provide at least one-half inch of additional space in the toe area. Arch supports or special devices within the shoe are absolutely unnecessary unless specially prescribed and fitted by a qualified person. Garments with built in foot covers (sometimes called "feet insides") can be useful, but again it's important the foot parts have enough room in them for growth and comfort.

As children begin to reach the crawling stages, clothes that protect them from injury become more important. However, the three earlier considerations for warmth, comfort, and cleanliness should not go by the wayside. Roomy, loose garments made from soft, natural fibers are best for this age. Overalls can be added to their wardrobes, and the knees of clothes can be reinforced with quilted pads to add durability as well as padding to these well-worn (both to body and fabric) areas. For outdoor wear, layers of clothing are more comfortable than large, bulky snow suits and constricting coats. Hoods help to keep bodies warm because they prevent heat from escaping through the head, and mittens form warm pockets for chilly fingers on the coldest days.

Fig. 12–2. The girls are happily dressed for a warm summer day in very light cotton clothes. The child on the left wears a wrap-around cotton top and drawstring shorts that fit very loosely over the legs. Her friend wears a cotton, pull-on, bubble dress that ties over the shoulders. Both kids are wearing canvas sneakers.

All these garments can be modified for kids as they get older. And clothing styles worn early in life such as sleepers and kimonos can be made in larger sizes for them.

Cotton corduroy coveralls or garments made from undyed denim make good, strong, and durable clothes for toddlers (eighteen months old). So do cotton shirts and stretch clothes. Clothes should be fastened with string-ties for easy changing and should be loose enough to allow for layering either with undershirts or sweaters.

Loose-fitting garments should be worn for sleepwear. The Consumer Products Safety Commission formed in 1972 enforces the 1953 Flammable Fabrics Act which has determined that all children's sleepwear (sizes 0 to 6x) must pass a standardized flammability test. Interestingly, diapers and underwear are exempt from the act. Additionally, children's sleepwear (excluding underwear), sizes 7 to 14, are also covered by the act, but less stringently. General wearing apparel must also meet certain flame-resistant standards.

In accordance with the act, fabrics were treated with chemical flame retardants, many of which have been proved seriously toxic to humans. One of these, TRIS, has been banned for use in children's sleepwear, but not for other general wearing apparel. Other man-made fibers have been developed that are made from inherently flame-resistant substances, but these too may prove to be dangerous to the wearers' bodies. Aside from this, these fibers are not comfortable, nor do they breathe or absorb bodily moisture properly.

Until our advanced technologies can produce effective, safe, and comfortable flame-retardant garments for children, we recommend that parents dress their children in natural fibers and increase their vigilance in terms of dangerous environmental factors in which fire is a part. Silk and wools do not burn readily and provide much more comfort and protection from the elements. They are durable, yet biodegradable, and interact naturally with a child's skin. Some man-made fibers, while flame retardant, melt when they are exposed to fire. They also can release toxic fumes when they burn. Natural fibers do not pose these problems.

During the ages between three and six, children seem to be at their most active. They have declared their independence and at-

Fig. 12–3. Here are two examples of overalls in different forms. The girl on the left wears appliquéd canvas pants, patched at the knee, over a striped cotton shirt. The smaller child is wearing a wrap-around, denim overall dress. Both of these garments fasten over the shoulders. Sandals and sneakers complete the outfit.

Fig. 12–4. *These playful kids are wearing durable clothes that lend themselves to action. The barefoot boy wears a cotton jogging suit. His playmate wears a great-looking, wide-wale corduroy jumpsuit that is knotted and fastened over the shoulders and gathered at the ankle. His feet are covered in soft leather booties, and he wears a boat-neck cotton t-shirt.*

tack everything about them with vigor and delight. Their clothing at this time should allow them all the freedom possible as well as protection from the environment. Though they may feel independent, they are still babies and need to be surrounded with warmth and comfort. Soft fibers are in order, as well as loose, well-fitting garments, especially for children's play clothes.

Body suits made from durable blends of wool and cotton are good clothes for children. These should be reinforced at the knees and elbows and fastened with string-ties. Elastic should be avoided around the waist because it applies too much pressure to the abdomen. Children do not need specific clothing fasteners at the waist, as their bodies are not fully delineated at this area. Clothes can fit loosely over the torso and be fastened over the shoulders.

Children's independent natures leave them with the often strongly expressed desire to dress themselves. Clothes should take this into account and be easy to put on. Unless they are large, buttons may be difficult for little fingers to maneuver. (However, learning to use buttons does encourage coordination and can add to the fun of kids' dressing.) Drawstrings are much easier for them to handle, and clothes that pull up over the legs and down over the head are best for growing kids. It's actually better for clothes to have fewer fasteners that may confuse and frustrate children. A simple tie or strap that loops over the shoulder — one that doesn't even need tying, but rather can be wriggled into — is best. A cautionary note on zippers: zippers should not be used for children's clothing because they can catch on skin, genitals, and fingers. Most garments don't need them at all, and anything worn close to the body should be soft, not cold and metallic.

A slight gathering at the ankle and wrists is helpful in kids' clothes to give gentle shaping to the clothes and to help keep the body warm. Armholes and necks should be wide to make dressing easier. Children should always have clean, undyed cotton underwear to wear, and it should be changed daily. For cooler weather, flannel and wool underclothes can also be worn.

Overalls are probably the best "overall" garment for children. They should be fastened over the shoulders and tied for easy wearing and be loose enough to allow for layering. Durable fabrics like cotton canvas, corduroy, and wool blends are good fabrics for overalls. For "dress up" these can be made from brushed cotton denim and velvet, which are attractive and durable. Soft cotton t-shirts, either with long or short sleeves are best worn with overalls. The feel of cotton is very nice on children's skins, not scratchy or irritating, and most kids will love these fabrics. They often complain, rightfully so, about the coarse, scratchy, or hot feel of synthetics. Their sensitive bodies welcome the feel of naturalness which cuddles them and makes them feel secure.

Several healthy clothing ideas have emerged from the recent physical fitness phenomenon of running. Many of the clothes developed for and by runners are comfortable and easy to wear. Sweatsuits, particularly, are excellent loose-fitting, body-conscious apparel that are great for kids. Drawstring sweatpants are easy to put on, durable, and wearable from fall through late spring. They can be layered over long cotton underwear in the cooler months. Sweatshirts come with hoods and pockets. These can be worn alone or over other clothes. Sweatsuits for kids can be made in strong cotton fabrics in many colors. Some styles we've seen have animal appliqués and designs printed in the fabrics, making the suits charming as well as functional. These clothes can also be made into dresses with drawstring waists and nightshirts. Active kids love the idea of clothes they can play in, and sweatsuits lend themselves to all sorts of activities.

For dress up, children's clothes should still hold true to the dictates of warmth, comfort, and cleanliness. A-line dresses in soft brushed cottons and corduroys can be very pretty and still comply with healthy concepts. Wrap-around skirts and jumpers layered over wool sweaters and cotton velour tops are excellent when worn with cotton tights in winter. Synthetic fibers should be particularly avoided for dress-up clothes because they are very warm and uncomfortable. Kids behave better when they feel well; their clothes should help them be happy in their environment, even if their activities must be restricted for a period of time.

Dress pants and overalls for both sexes are delightful when

Fig. 12–5. *The pretty A-line dress is 100 percent cotton flannel. The shape of the dress falls from the shoulders naturally. The purse is made from the same fabric and is worn over the shoulder. Cotton socks and soft leather Mary Jane shoes complete the look.*

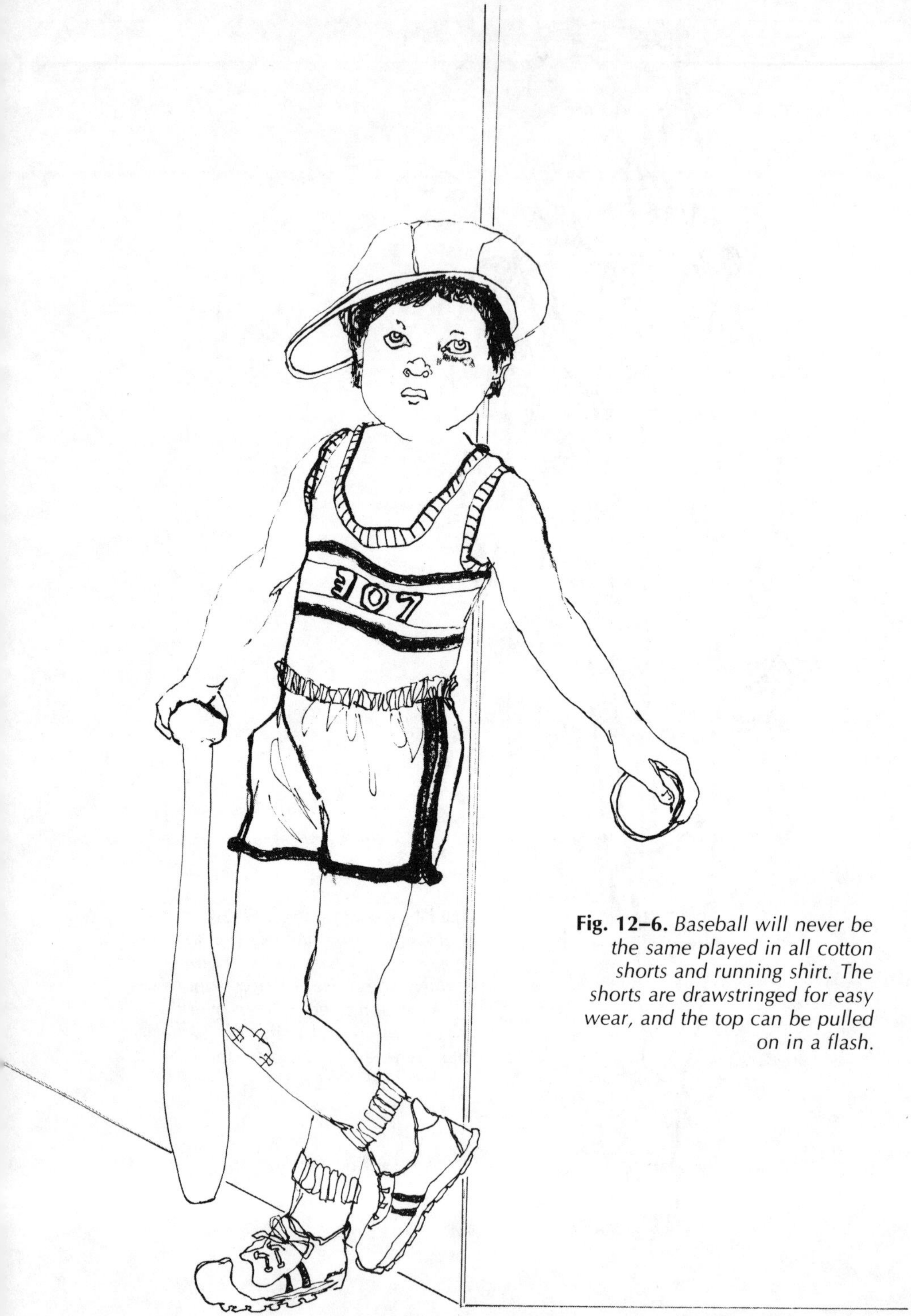

Fig. 12–6. *Baseball will never be the same played in all cotton shorts and running shirt. The shorts are drawstringed for easy wear, and the top can be pulled on in a flash.*

made from brushed natural fibers. If a suit is required for a child, healthy dressing principles should be remembered. Waistbands must not bind, and pants should be held up by suspenders, not belts. Jackets should be loose and unstructured so they don't constrict the child's arms. Ties are very uncomfortable and unnecessary for young children. Open collars and sweaters are much healthier and comfortable. Appliqued and embroidered clothes are very natural and attractive on children, and kids love anything that personalizes an article of clothes for them.

Short pants and coveralls are great for kids in summer. These can be made from cotton denim, corduroy, or cotton canvas. We recommend clothes that are not heavily dyed for kids. Several good types of coveralls are on the market in strong durable cottons in natural colors. These get softer with repeated washings and last for ages. Patches make them even more charming and preserve vulnerable areas.

It's extremely important to protect children's skin from too much sun. Young skin is much more susceptible to the sun's harmful radiation. Although kids may look adorable when they're bronzed and look like berries, there is experimental evidence that too much exposure to the sun can cause eventual skin cancer. It is unthinkable that in the interest of making the child look cute a parent could subject the child to the potential for developing a malignancy later in life. For the summer, some kind of light cotton cover is a good idea to protect children's bodies. This is particularly important when they are swimming, since water reflects the sun's rays and may cause a severe burn. Also, children should not sit around too long in wet swimsuits because germs can breed in a warm, moist environment and cause rashes on the bottom or generate infections in the genital area.

Common sense should be used in these instances and those caring for children should be aware of how clothing can affect health, especially in play situations. Kids who play on a rough terrain need more clothing protection than those who play on grassland. Children who spend time in concrete playgrounds require durable clothes that can stand up to falls and protect knees, elbows, and skins from scrapes. Those who pursue artistic activities, such as dance, need to dress appropriately and comfortably, and kids who like nothing better than to curl up and read a book should feel good in their clothes as well.

When young children are involved in outdoor activities and having fun throwing snowballs, building forts, sledding, and tobogganing, they have little care for what they are wearing. Kids will rarely complain of discomfort when they are having a good time; but tired, wet, overexposed bodies are susceptible to colds, flu, and pneumonia, and the chilly hike home from the playground may be all that's needed to expose a tired child to the possibility of illness. It's essential that they be provided with warm clothing so they won't be exposed to the cold. Layering clothes for warmth is the best way to keep kids comfortable and healthy in winter. Quilted cotton corduroy jackets and down-filled vests are lightweight but very warm and help retain body heat. Again, coveralls, especially with drawstrings at the ankle to keep in warmth, are excellent clothes in stormy weather. Long underwear, preferably made from wool lined with cotton or flannel, with sweaters and overalls layered over them, protect the body and keep it comfortably dry. A down-filled or quilted jacket adds a light-weight warmth, and in weather that's cool but not wet, a down-filled vest that keeps the torso warm may be sufficient for the active child.

As mentioned before, the best head covering in cold weather for everyone is a hood that attaches to the jacket. This will keep the back of the neck warm and prevent cold air from chilling the upper back and shoulders. A woolen scarf crossed over the chest adds additional warmth and comfort, and mittens keep hands nice and warm. For less active wear, wool coats worn over sweaters are adequate. Legs should be covered, and feet protected from the elements in well-fitting, waterproofed, leather boots. If a lot of time is spent outdoors in snow, fleece-lined boots worn over wool socks are best for keeping feet warm and dry.

Parents begin to worry about shoes when their children reach the toddler stage. Ideally, it would be best for kids to go barefoot (except on dangerous surfaces, like city streets) until they reach

Fig. 12–7. The girl on the left wears a down-filled, patchwork, cotton vest over a long-sleeved, cotton, turtle-neck sweater and pull-on corduroy pants, which wrap around on the top and button diagonally. Her boots are fleece-lined leather, ankle high. Her little friend is wearing a quilted, corduroy, kimono-type wrap jacket over a cotton shirt and wool pants that are gathered at the ankles and tied. She wears laced, leather walking shoes.

school age. This would give their feet a chance to develop naturally and not be pressured, literally, into the structure of a shoe. Their feet would be anatomically correct, and muscles and tendons could develop to their fullest potential. Because the terrain on which most of us must walk is hard concrete, kids' feet need the protection of shoes earlier than age six or seven, but this needn't hamper healthy foot development. A little careful consideration given to kids' shoes can go a long way toward ensuring their feet will be healthy.

These considerations include checking for tightness, seams inside the shoes, hardware that can chafe the toes, hard, inflexible, leather uppers that don't allow the feet to bend, and improper heel heights. Normal feet do not need special arch or ankle support, and children's shoes should not be specially designed to force the foot into any particular form. Putting a growing foot into a corrective shoe may cause it to diminish in strength. This would cause a severe handicap in later years, particularly if the child has athletic interests that require strong ankle muscles. It's also important to note that if a child complains about shoes, chances are the shoes hurt and are uncomfortable. Kids usually are not too articulate in explaining why something bothers them, particularly when it comes to their clothes, so some sleuthing may be necessary to get to the bottom of complaints. Careful investigation, however, will pay off. Your kids' feet, and ultimately your kids, will thank you for vigilance in ensuring their shoes fit.

Sneakers and jogging shoes made from canvas breathe and stretch with the feet. These tend to wear out quickly but are less expensive than leather shoes, so they can be replaced more often. Sandals are great for kids in summer because they free the toes for growth and stretching. Although there may be some peer pressure to wear high heels and clogs, it is not advisable for young children to wear anything that inhibits muscle action or shortens their tendons. Wearing high heels distorts the bones of the feet and can cause severe foot damage and pinched nerves. Parents do know what's best for kids; although some compromises may be made as far as clothing choices are concerned, parents must put their feet down, literally, when it comes to kids' shoes. Our feet connect us with the earth. Kids' feet must give them a firm base on which to grow.

Children learn about their world as soon as they begin to touch it, as soon as it begins to touch them. Messages are transmitted prenatally about what life feels like. After they are born infants learn and grow very rapidly, hopefully in a healthy, warm, and loving environment. Every inch of their bodies responds to stimuli, unjaded by experience, totally open to the newness of the world. Helping kids to develop healthy dressing attitudes as well as techniques for applying the concepts to their lives can go a long way in aiding them to develop holistic, environmentally healthy attitudes about their world. Self-sufficiency is important for survival and an awareness of dressing — not just because society demands we wear clothes, but because it is an important aspect of health and bodily protection — is an important lesson for kids to learn. The generations that follow us will be the ones that effect healthful changes for our planet. Giving kids the wherewithal, the tools for evolving, is a great gift we should all afford.

Helpful Hints For Choosing Kids' Clothes

- Always allow kids to help shop for their clothes. If they have a say in the choices, they'll be happier in the clothes.
- Find shops that understand kids' ideas and moods.
- Some children's clothes may require alterations. If you are not adept with a needle, make sure the clothing store can do it for you.
- Children should try clothes on before they are purchased. Have them move around and play a bit to see if the clothes are comfortable.
- Never buy anything that binds or chafes or seems a little tight for a child. Children grow bigger, not smaller.
- Dress children in the colors and fabrics of the season. Train them to understand their bodies' functions so they know they should dress for comfort and protection, in accordance with climatic conditions.
- Always allow for breathing room as well as growing room in kids' clothes.

- Be less concerned with kids' wearing clothes that "match". If a child chooses a bright orange kimono shirt to wear with her fire engine red coveralls, she probably has a good reason. The colors may provide the "up" she needs for playing.

- Creativity can only develop if it is encouraged. If children see their parents do healthy things, their imaginations will take the activities a step farther. When kids dress up to be like Mommy and Daddy — clomping around in Dad's well-worn Birkenstocks and wearing Mom's soft woolen caftan are just the right things for them to imitate.

- Allowing kids to dress themselves encourages independence and self-awareness. Children should not feel alienated from what they wear. They really love to choose for themselves; if they are given a good example, they can do very well for themselves.

13

Designs for Living

Creating a wardrobe for day-to-day living can be an exciting experience filled with creativity and innovation. Because natural fibers provide such a marvelous array of textures, all of the clothes we have chosen for our natural dressers' wardrobes are made from cotton, linen, silk, or wool. Since clothes are needed for work as well as play, we've included designs that can go to work and still be healthy and comfortable.

Environmental awareness in the workplace is growing with the introduction of safety regulations; because of the problems of conservation, an awareness of dressing with the environment of the workplace will also become more important. If there is not enough electricity to power the huge air conditioners needed to cool a large high-rise building, different types of clothes from those traditionally worn in offices will have to be designed. The same holds true in cold weather. Limited fuel supplies may mean colder offices. But the concept of layering lends itself perfectly to these problems, and so do the natural fibers that retain body heat and keep us comfortable.

Drawstring pants and a cotton shirt lend themselves well to a

Fig. 13–1. *The natural dresser wears an all-white, all-cotton outfit. The umbrella is paper.* (Photos for this chapter, except where noted, by Mats Nordström)

comfortable, casual look; but they are also suitable for a relaxed work atmosphere (fig. 13–2). In many formal settings, suits for men are the bastion of tradition, particularly in western civilization. However, by loosening the jacket a bit and giving it an unstructured, body-conscious fit, the jacket becomes more comfortable and healthy. Coupled with loose trousers, held up by suspenders rather than a tight belt, the suit is much more suitable for natural dressers (fig. 13–3).

Success-oriented women have been encouraged of late to don the armor of their male counterparts in order to look the part of a successful business person. However, women can wear a loose, unstructured jacket, t-shirt top and wrap skirt and still look "professional", while they look healthy. Figure 13–4 shows a suit in a linen and cotton blend.

Made in different fabrics, one design that can adapt to work wear as well as to leisure wear is the karate suit (fig. 13–5, left). For summer, the wrap jacket and drawstring pants can be made of cotton. For a more elegant look, linen or silk can be used; in winter, corduroy or wool jersey would be an excellent choice. Whatever the season, these designs have been created to be versatile. The drawing on the right in figure 13–5 shows a simple A-line dress that can be worn sashed, or under a coat made from the same fabric in spring and summer, and layered over pants for fall and winter. This style can be worn in the office or for leisure, depending on the fabric. Blouses can be worn in any season — made from wool, silk, or voile. They can be worn with wrap skirts, drawstring pants, or wrap-waist pants (fig. 13–6).

Another possibility for women is a simple A-line, shoulder-supported dress made in soft cotton, tied at the waist with an obi, and worn under a loose cotton, cardigan jacket (fig. 13–7). Figure 13–7 (right) shows a sundress made from hand-dyed cotton. Again, it uses the shoulders to support the lines and is belted loosely at the waist.

Wrap dresses are perhaps the most comfortable of all. The long dress shown in figure 13–8 is made from cotton fabric that has been hemmed. The top is tacked together over the shoulders, and the

Fig. 13–2. *Drawstring pants and shirt (Left,* courtesy of Putumayo, New York; *above,* courtesy of Three Wishes, New York)

Fig. 13–3. *Prototype design for men's suit.* (All fashion illustrations for this chapter by Curt Wagner.)

Fig. 13–4. *Linen suit.* (Courtesy of Three Wishes, New York)

Fig. 13–5. The figure on the left shows the versatile karate suit. It can be worn throughout the year, fashioned from different fabrics. The figure on the right wears a cotton dress worn layered over pants and under a wrap-around coat.

Fig. 13–6. *Wool or silk dolman-sleeved shirts look great loosely bloused with wrap-waisted wool pants.*

Fig. 13–7. *Above, cotton wrap dress* (Courtesy of Tamala Design with Bagel, New York). *Right, the versatile sundress made in soft cotton* (Courtesy Putumayo, New York). *Made in a lustrous silk, both dresses would be appropriate for evening wear.*

Fig. 13–8. *Cotton wrap dress.* (Photo by Joe Roschko)

Fig. 13–9. *Silk or wool jersey evening dress. It can also be made as a long evening skirt wrapped at the hip.*

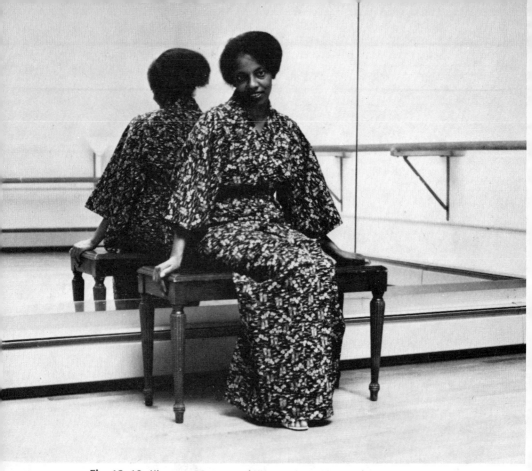

Fig. 13–10. *Kimono.* (Courtesy of Kimono-tique, New York)

dress is sashed with a belt made from the same material as the dress. The easy flow of this dress makes it comfortable for either a party dress or a casual, lounge garment. One very easy dress for evening wear wraps around the body, under the arms, and ties over the bosom, sarong style. It can be made from silk or wool jersey, and a matching shawl can be added to provide a warm cover-up (fig. 13–9).

For both at-home and evening wear, one of the most elegant and at the same time comfortable garments ever made is the kimono. The model in figure 13–9 is wearing one made from cotton. Formal kimonos can be made from heavily embroidered silks with beautiful designs and traditional motifs.

It is perhaps easiest to dress for casual living, but all of the following clothes can be adapted for other times as well. The suit in figure 13–11 is made from silk, drawstring, straight-legged pants, a silk camisole, and a quilted, hand-dyed silk jacket. It can be worn dressed up or down depending on the occasion. A bat-wing smock is suitable for men and women and looks great over Berber, harem, or drawstring pants. A dressy fabric, such as silk, makes it appropriate for more formal occasions.

A modernized version of the caftan can be worn as an overcoat in formal occasions or as a leisure robe. Elaborate decorations can make this garment extremely elegant, while simple fabrics and design give it a comfortable and healthful look.

The handsome sweater in the photograph (fig. 13–11, left) is hand-knitted from hand-dyed wools. This sweater is suitable for men or women, and its natural look coordinates well with other

Fig. 13–11. *Silk suit.* (Courtesy of Tamala Design with Bagel)

Fig. 13–12. *Above, a hand-knit sweater; right, a Guatemala hulepa* (Courtesy of Putumayo, New York).

clothes. The beautiful Guatemalan *hulepa,* a cotton overshirt, is functional as well as comfortable. It serves as a cover-up, a protector from the elements, and a becoming garment. (See figure 13–12, right.)

Natural dressers can choose a variety of designs and fabrics to help them dress healthily. The fun lies in combining their own ideas with those already on the market. Inventing new designs for dressing can add to the charm of creating a healthy wardrobe. Freedom of movement in clothes can help a person feel freer in mind as well as body. Any clothes that allow this freedom are clothes for the natural dresser.

Part 3

14

Labels

One of the best aids one can have in learning to dress for health lies in clothing labels. Labels identify the product and provide information about its care. A carefully worded instructional label can help the consumer make intelligent clothing selections, particularly if the consumer is alerted to what to look for in labeling. Less importantly, labels serve as advertisements for the clothing's manufacturer or designer.

Currently mandated by law, clothing labels have not always been necessary. In fact, for centuries product identification and care information were virtually unnecessary since the fibers used were limited to a few simple ones — wool, cotton, linen, and silk. Cleaning methods were even simpler — soap (homemade from animal and plant fats and lye gleaned from the ashes of wood fires) and water provided all the cleansing power necessary.

The early Egyptians washed their sparkling, white linen garments in the Nile River and laid them along its banks to dry and bleach in the sun. This early clothesline technique persisted for thousands of years. Generation after generation washed its clothes in rivers, lakes, or tubs of stream water and used the renewable energy of the sun to finish the laundering process. Interestingly, even modern technology must acquiesce to the desirability of sun-dried clothes that smell fresh and clean. Every detergent, fabric-softener, and bleach manufacturer tries to claim that its products impart to laundry the same fresh, outdoor smell and feel that the sun provides. Claims are one thing, but nothing beats the sun.

When the petrochemical industry entered into textile production in the twentieth century, a whole field of chemically produced soaps, now called detergents, emerged. Detergents are an example of how an unnatural, synthetic product has replaced a natural, organic one. Environmentally, detergent production and use has been devastating. Soap is inherently biodegradable. It is developed from natural substances and returns back to the earth broken down by bacteria that attack the animal or plant fat used to produce the soap. Detergents, on the other hand, are synthesized from petroleum in a process that requires intense heat and the interaction of other chemicals such as chlorine, which contains mercury — a highly toxic substance. Other chemicals are then added to soften water or bleach fibers. It is estimated that the stress placed on the environment in terms of this pollution is close to three times greater for detergent production than it is for soap production.

Some detergents are not attacked by bacteria in the ecosystem. Because of this, detergent foam has appeared in streams. Other detergents are biodegradable. However, to make a detergent biodegradable, benzene must be added. Unfortunately, in water benzene can convert to phenol, a highly toxic and caustic substance that kills fish and other aquatic life when it enters the ecosystem. Benzene-based products are harmful to the individual consumer who uses them in home washing machines. Phenol can be absorbed through the skin or breathed from the atmosphere. It is highly toxic to humans.

Phosphates are also added to detergents because they soften water and suspend dirt particles, which can then be rinsed away. Phosphates, too, are ecologically unsound. They stimulate the growth of algae in water systems, which in turn clog the waterways with organic matter. To combat this problem, some detergents contain nitrilotri-acetic acid (NTA) as a replacement for phosphate. This substance has caused birth defects in laboratory animals and enters the ecosystem as readily as the other chemicals.

In actuality, detergents clean no better than plain, ordinary soap; unfortunately, they've done a terrible job in dirtying up our environment. The rationale is that new, man-made textiles require new, man-made soaps to clean them.

Because of the complex chemical structure of the new fabrics, it was difficult for even highly trained launderers to determine what type of cleaning solution was best for them. Care labels became necessary when fabrics were ruined in the wash. They became mandatory when it became obvious that both the reputations of the man-made textile industry as well as its satellite products could be blackened if these wonder fabrics either couldn't get clean or were destroyed in the process!

The Federal Trade Commission's Permanent Care Labeling Rule was enacted in 1972 to resolve the question of how to clean delicate fabrics. These labels must inform the consumer about regular care and maintenance to be observed in the ordinary, daily use of a garment including washing, drying, ironing, bleaching, and dry cleaning. They must also warn the consumer of any normal procedure that might usually be applied to the type of fabric that may actually harm it. These labels must be readily accessible to the consumer and describe the potential shrinkage of an article of clothing. (If a garment shrinks more than the amount stated on the label, the manufacturer may be sued for libel.)

Other mandatory labeling information must include the fiber content and the percentages of each fiber used — along with the name and identifying information about the manufacturer. This is particularly important for natural dressers who wish to ensure they are purchasing the best quality, healthy fibers in their clothing.

Because labels must list fiber content and percentages, natural dressers can choose natural fibers and natural blends, the first step toward healthy dressing. The fiber percentages listed must be made in order of weight, if the weight of the fiber is more than 5 percent of the total. This can be particularly important in choosing a blend that may include some synthetic fibers. Choose the garment with the higher percentage of natural fibers rather than a blend that is predominantly man-made.

The Textile Products Identification Act was introduced in 1960 to protect consumers from false advertising in the fiber content of textile products. This was unnecessary before the introduction of synthetics because natural fibers are easier to determine by look, feel, and texture. However, man-made fibers are hard to distinguish from one another. In fact, it is impossible to determine what acrylics, polyesters, nylons, and other man-made fibers are constructed from by look, feel, or texture. The TFPI Act has some disadvantages in that the labels do not define, because of the technical nature, the components of synthetics. Neither are the dyes listed. Because all of these ingredients are made from a technology that harms the environment, and many of the chemicals are hazardous to humans, a wise consumer should avoid purchasing clothes made from synthetic fibers. It's important to read between the lines of a label and realize what it doesn't tell you may hurt you.

The Wool Products Labeling Act was enacted in 1939. It states that any wool garment label must include the amount of wool contained in a fabric, the percent by weight of new wool in the garment, the percent of reused or reprocessed fibers used, and the percent of fibers other than wool used (if more than 5 percent of total weight). It must also state any aggregate of other fibers as well as any nonfibrous fibers that may be in the garment. Part of the information contained in these labels are classifications of types of wool fibers.

Wool: new or virgin wool fiber that has never been manufactured into cloth before.

Reprocessed Wool: fiber that has been reclaimed and remanufactured from wool materials never used before. Often these are taken from clippings and scraps salvaged during the manufacture of wool products.

Reused Wool: fiber that has been salvaged from wool materials previously used, including old clothing and other products previously worn. Reused wool is usually blended with new fibers. The product is less durable and less attractive than the other wool garments but also less costly.

Labels are not required to mention the type of sheep the wool comes from; but if the wool is from a particularly fine breed, such as a merino, it will most likely mention it.

The Fur Products Labeling Act was enacted in 1957 and amended in 1961. It requires that the name of the animal and country of origin be affixed to the garment.

There are also voluntary labels. Basically these labels attest to the chemical and technological capabilities of the product according to the manufacturer's standards. The qualities standardized are breaking and tearing strength, colorfastness, seam strength, absence of odor and dimensional changes after laundering. These all refer to features of the garment other than the fabric itself. No voluntary standards are set for breathability, comfort, texture, feel, or other healthful qualities.

If the garments comply with the Voluntary Industry Standards, the label may have one or more of the following designations: USASI (for United States American Standards Institute), AATT (for American Association for Textile Technology), ASTM (for American Society for Testing and Materials), AATCC (for American Association of Textile Chemists and Colorists), and IFI (for International Fabricare Institute). These are the seals of approval of the garment's own manufacturer, not the objective, standardized opinions of consumer groups or laboratories. They are merely another form of advertisement that claims a garment will do what the other advertisements say it will. Informed consumers should be aware that these kinds of labels are public relations presentations — really a waste of the paper they're printed on.

Some voluntary labels include such additional information as special finishes and fabric structure. They may also discuss the quality of the fabric. They may include information about mercerization (to give cotton fibers added strength and luster) and sanforization, which means the fabric will shrink no more than 1 percent. These labels are helpful in further understanding the care a fabric may require or can attest to the quality of the fibers used. For example, if the label reads "Pima cotton", the consumer can be assured that the finest grade of cotton was used for the garment. If a label describes the place of origin of the fiber, the choice is much easier for an aware consumer. It would be far more intelligent for consumers to demand that labels require more of this information rather than more advertisements that bedeck almost all clothes on today's market. Unfortunately, this information is not mandatory and usually only expensive garments will discuss (literally brag about) the fine quality of its fibers.

Brand labels contain the distinctive design or hallmarks that identify a manufacturer or designer. The most recognizable brand labels today are those found on the back pockets of jeans or any other signature that appears on sleeves, lapels, or somewhere else on the garment. Of course, some brands have better reputations than others, and some consumers feel assured that their favorite manufacturer always makes the same high-quality goods over and over. However, it's better to count on your own judgment than that of the manufacturer. Always check clothes for workmanship, feel, and look. Even the best brands slip up from time to time. The best quality controller is the consumer.

Certification labels indicate that a garment has been tested by an independent (from the manufacturer) laboratory. Union labels ostensibly assure the consumer that the garment has been made under safe working conditions. However, these do not indicate whether or not the garment is ecologically safe in its manufacturing process or if it is ultimately safe to the consumer.

Good Housekeeping, Consumer Reports, and *Parents Magazine* have standards on which they base their seals of approval. These attest to a garment's workmanship and general appearance, as well as its economic value relative to similar products. If one of these organizations does not approve of a garment, something is seriously wrong with it.

There are several rules of thumb that careful consumers can use for judicious, effective label reading. To begin with, healthy clothes

don't require complicated labels full of complicated terminology —
just as good nutritious food doesn't involve complicated chemical
names. If cleaning instructions appear long and complicated, the
fabric contains chemicals — as well as the accompanying dangers
that can occur with chemical use (or misuse!). Avoid clothes that
require elaborate cleaning procedures. Natural fibers do not require
special procedures; care for these fabrics is clear and straightfor-
ward.

Read labels to determine if harmful processes or finishes have
been applied to the fabric. It should be remembered that if one
makes a mistake washing a natural fabric, the only thing ruined is
the garment. Toxins are not released the way they may be with
synthetics.

Be aware of the environment. If strong detergents, fabric softeners (which are, incidentally, recommended for synthetics because they reduce static in these fibers), and other chemicals must be
applied to keep a garment clean, avoid its use. It's far better for the
environment to wash a cotton garment in a mild soap three times
than to wash a synthetic one once in a chemical solution that
pollutes the ecosystem (and ultimately your own body). Who wants
to drink algae or detergent foam?

Finally, use labels as a place to begin changing your wardrobe
to a healthier one for your body. Read about the contents of your
clothes as you would about the contents of the food you eat to
nourish your body and the books you read to nourish your mind.
Demand that labels give all the information about clothes, not just
what a manufacturer cares to advertise about the product. Read
through the lines — all the small print — especially when it comes to
children's clothes and nightwear. Try to avoid anything that's confusing or complicated. Clothes should be a joy to wear, not ecologi-
cal time bombs that can cause misery and discomfort in the future.

15

The first steps

It was predawn one early spring day that we were introduced to one of the healthiest, most comfortable and comforting dress for health principles we have encountered. We were visiting an ashram (a yoga retreat) in upstate New York and guests were invited to welcome the day with a series of yoga asanas (postures). It was cold and dark when the wake-up gong sounded, and the thought of getting out of a warm bed was not pleasant. However, seasoned visitors and residents alike got around this by wrapping their blankets, still warm from their bodies' heat, around themselves as they rose, still drowsy, to await the yoga instructor and the sunrise.

We each draped one light blanket around our shoulders and joined the others in the large meditation room overlooking the valley and lake below. Rather than becoming chilled, our bodies remained warm and relaxed and waking up became a gentle transition, not a harsh jolt that is received when a stimulating activity suddenly follows a relaxed one. The blankets did not encumber our actions or postures, but rather lent a kind of grace to our movements. As the morning's exercises progressed in difficulty, our bodies easily adapted to the pace because our muscles remained warm and relaxed. Soon we were feeling comfortable enough to dispense with the blankets. We continued the session in comfortable, loose clothing, keeping the blankets aside for a covering during meditation.

Of course, in an environment that encourages relaxation and contented living, such as an ashram, using one's bed clothes to keep warm during exercise is quite natural. Yet this practice can be adapted to everyday life. Instead of jolting the body up in the morning, consider taking one of the covers with you as you make the transition from sleep to wakefulness. Even if you keep it around you for only a few minutes your body will have a chance to adapt more readily to the pace of the day if it is introduced to activity in a relaxed manner.

Which leads us to the feasibility of adapting the ideas of dressing for health to everyday life. Many people work in an environment in which strict dress codes are enforced. However, there are ways of getting around them. Some dress regulations can be relaxed when an individual is working on a project alone, or away from the general work area, or by people who do not come into contact with clients or customers on a daily basis. The aid of supervisors and employers can be enlisted in the quest for healthier dressing conditions. This may make them aware that their health is at stake too. Relaxation should not be equated with laxity or looseness of mind or attitude. People who breathe well, work well; a comfortable work environment will enable people to maximize the efficiency of their performance.

Some years ago, one of us worked at a large urban department store during the Christmas rush season. Because the store was rather stately and dignified, a strict dress code was in force, and we learned all the rules during an orientation period. A group of salespersons were assigned to a veteran in each department, who showed us the ropes and acquainted us with stock and selling techniques. Our group was assigned to an attractive, middle-aged woman who was impeccably dressed in basic black wool — impeccably save for her feet, which were covered by a pair of well-worn, cushion-soled,

old-fashioned walking shoes that made her look as if she were
standing on marshmallow puffs. Our group giggled behind hands as
we noticed these shoes, but our teacher nonchalantly commented
that she'd like to see what we would be putting on our feet after
running up and down to stockrooms and catering to demanding
customers in the busiest department on the floor. In less than a week
she was vindicated. Those of us who could walk at all were wearing
the most comfortable and seemingly out-of-place foot coverings we
could find. Foot-soaking became a way of life for all of us, and we
had an initiation into dressing, at least in part, a bit more healthily
and comfortably. We also had better sales tallies in the long run
because we could move faster and were less grumpy!

To dress for health one needn't go cold turkey and immediately
take to wearing caftans and togas, giving up all one's earthly synthetic possessions for the sake of the flax plant. Dressing for health
can be accomplished gradually and in some ways quietly. (This can
be particularly helpful for natural dressers who still feel they must
remain "in the closet" by dressing healthily only when surrounded
by those who understand their inclinations.)

Begin at the office and take a few minutes a day to undo your
cuffs and collar and remove your shoes, jackets, and sweaters. Better
still, wear loose clothes — not ones that hang — but rather ones that
allow for freedom of movement. Try wearing underwear made from
soft natural fibers. Boxer shorts are better for men than jockey shorts,
and women's underpants should be made from cotton — or at least
have a cotton shield in the crotch. Elasticized socks and support
hose can seriously restrict circulation and should be worn only
when a serious vein condition calls for them. Loose ankle socks are
much better, and natural hose for women (expensive, but durable
and becoming more available) are a better choice than nylon pantyhose. Keep comfortable shoes to change into during rest periods,
lunch time, or during coffee breaks. (Even a half-hour break in
which you change your shoes, loosen your collar, belt, or blouse
can be a refreshing boost to your body.)

Wearing a vest is a good idea in cooler weather because
layering may obviate the need for heavy overcoats particularly if

Fig. 15–1. *A roomy, lightweight wool sweater worn with heavy cotton canvas pants that are cut comfortably are great for hiking.* (Drawings for this chapter by Curt Wagner.)

you're going in and out of heated buildings and chilly outdoors. The body adapts better to climatic changes when clothing is layered. Keep a comfortable sweater or jacket in your office for cooler days.

Color coordinate your clothes. Have a comfortable, color-coordinated jacket made to go with your more regimented suits or looser pants to go with more tailored jackets. A tailor or seamstress can be an invaluable ally in developing a flexible, healthy wardrobe. Though it can appear expensive at the outset, having a matching garment to coordinate and interchange with your good work clothes make health dressing transitions easy and painless. As people become accustomed to seeing you dress in an easier fashion they'll get used to the idea of your healthy dressing outlook and accept it more readily.

The important thing is to be comfortable in your clothes — even if at times you must wear some unhealthy ones. Being conscious of healthy dressing principles and wearing healthy clothes as often as possible lead to healthier dressing habits. For example, suspenders can be considered either faddish or sedate since they're worn by both disco dancers and investment bankers alike. The design of the pattern or the colors will distinguish what type to wear, but they are healthy items and can adapt to most lifestyles. Wrap-around shirts can be made from cottons for a casual look or heavier wools or fine silks for a more business-oriented, successful look. A wrap-around fastened at the waist with a clasp or button is more dignified than a tied bow — but the health principle is there regardless of the way the shirt is fastened.

Wearing a shirt with a collar one-quarter size larger than usual need not look slovenly, especially if the result is more comfort and less pressure and chafing around the neck area. The wearer will appear much more confident and less harried than a trussed-up, starch-collared counterpart whose face is beet-red from neck restriction.

Sleeves that are designed for easy roll-up are also good, everyday, work-wear investments. Soft cottons lend themselves well to rolling, and some shirts have special loops and buttons that hold the sleeves in place when rolled.

Another important aspect of dressing for health is avoiding synthetic fibers. Natural fibers allow the body to breathe and perspire naturally. Nobody should wear a steambath suit in an already over-heated office. Synthetics can contribute to heat exhaustion and discomfort and decrease work efficiency (as well as make for a lot of discontent) in an office situation. Natural fibers also have a richer, more important look and feel for those who are interested in the status their clothing gives them.

Most importantly, a healthy person is a confident one. Confidence does not lie in a suit of clothes, but in what one does for the clothes. Conservation of energy in clothing may be as effective a tool in advancement as any of the edicts of dressing for success. Although some kind of armor may be necessary to protect the body for battle, clothes should not be worn to protect people from inter-human relationships.

Healthy clothes should correspond with the work that has to be done. Wataru Ohashi explained to us a Japanese principle of dress for TPO: or Time, Place, and Occasion. In other words, clothes should have a specific meaning for a particular time of day, a place such as business or home, and an occasion, such as a job or a party. Clothing should suit these criteria.

Many people we have spoken with have commented that if they are too dressed up, they can't get any work done because they're too conscious of what they are wearing: some are concerned they may soil the suit or tear it, while others feel too restricted to move about freely. Perhaps this is a carry-over from childhood when we were told not to play in the mud when we were wearing our Sunday best.

Conversely, being underclad for a particular situation or likewise inappropriately dressed may seriously hamper work and achievement. Sitting around in a bathrobe, though comfortable, may not be conducive to carrying on the day's business. It's difficult to carry on conversations with others if you're always worried about modesty or some other clothing problem. Hence, healthy clothes are appropriate ones. To get a job done, wear what goes best with that job.

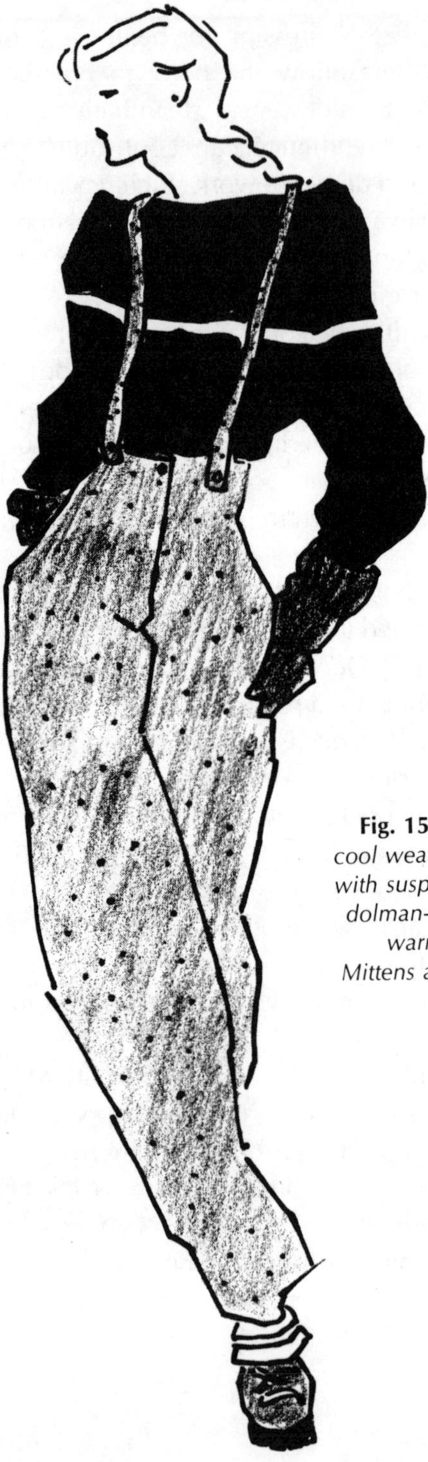

Fig. 15–2. For outdoor work or play in cool weather, baggy wool tweed trousers with suspenders worn over a heavy wool dolman-sleeve sweater provide comfort, warmth, and freedom of movement. Mittens are good if you're outdoors for a long period of time.

People who have their own businesses, or who freelance, are aware that self-motivation is very important. Part of this lies in dressing for the greatest energy efficiency for the job at hand. Sometimes donning a strong pair of overalls is all that's needed to stimulate a desire to finish painting a room, cleaning the floor, or writing the final chapter. Wearing favorite clothes can also affect our behavior. A special, old, worn-out sweater when you are sad can help to comfort you, or wearing a smashing red kimono may give you confidence to make an important decision.

Clothes interact with the spirit, the body, the soul, and the mind. Each part of the person is affected by what that person wears. Dressing healthily can make these aspects interact harmoniously — clothes must fit the person, not the other way around.

Dressing for Business

One of the most desirable characteristics of a successful business person is flexibility. Natural dressing lends itself to this and makes for comfortably successful and attractive people. Comfort is contagious; if you look comfortable you can help make others so. Natural dressers are not children dressed up to look like adults. They are in control of their dress situations. This comfortable, self-assured attitude makes natural dressers assertive but not threatening.

The image of a macho-power-tripping individual is often exemplified by a carefully chiseled male wearing a carefully tailored get-up — clothes and looks to intimidate and control those around him. Intimidation has worked very well in our world and has left its mark in ravaged lands as well as on ravaged people. A truly effective and powerful person is unassuming, pleasant to be with, not aggressive or chauvinistically assertive. Aggressive conformity is the result of insecurity.

Yet even comfortable looking and feeling people can get uptight and nervous. Stress and tension can be greatly relieved by proper breathing and comfortable posture. Healthy clothes can help a person get through stressful times with very little wear and tear.

Clothes can also impart a sense of security. Some people like to

Fig. 15–3. *A tailored suit need not be constricting. This wool wrap skirt and raglan-sleeved jacket provides a business outfit that is comfortable and suitable for the boardroom.*

wear a piece of jewelry or a good-luck necktie that reminds them of pleasurable times and experiences or friends and lovers. A friend of ours who holds a high-power position at a brokerage firm always carries a smooth round stone in one of the pockets of his suits. Whenever he gets tense or uptight he fingers the stone in his pocket for a few minutes. It reminds him of the mountains where he found it and soothes him so he can continue his work, less tense.

Staying in the same clothes all day, sometimes for as long as fifteen hours, is much too long. We suggest changing some item of what you wear as often as possible during the day. Some companies have exercise programs for employees because they were found to increase mental acuity and work efficiency. People change into exercise clothes or loosen their regular work clothes during this period, and the change does them a lot of good. If the sessions are scheduled later in the day before people leave work, they can often travel home in clothes different from the ones they wore in the morning. This breaks up a long work day and gives the person an impression of change, even if there hasn't been a major one.

Many therapists recommend that people take vacations periodically to break up intense work activity. Sometimes it's difficult to take time off, so some meditate daily to clear their minds and take a mental trip elsewhere. Just changing clothes as a person travels from place to place in a day can affect a significant enough daily change to break up the monotony of work. Having different clothes for different activities also helps. Most of us wouldn't dream of sleeping in our suits — nightwear is usually looser and more comfortable. The same can hold true for any leisure time we have in a day — loosen up, change for an hour, even if it's just your shoes. You'll feel much better.

There are other techniques for making transitions to natural and healthful dressing. It's important to understand personal needs, but it is equally important to understand environmental situations as well. It's helpful to know something about how the climate and weather affects your body. Admittedly weather forecasts are far from accurate, but as your body becomes more in tune with your environment, you'll become more aware of daily climatic changes and

Fig. 15−4. *Drawstring pants in a heavy wool fabric are gathered at the ankles with pull tabs to keep the body warm. The wool jacket has roomy sleeves so shirts and sweaters fit comfortably underneath. A cashmere scarf keeps the neck warm.*

can do your own forecasting with a little help from meteorologists. You'll soon be able to judge that you shouldn't wear your tightest shoes on a very hot day because feet expand in the heat, and tight shoes will make your feet hurt.

Bodies also expand in hot, humid weather. Don't wear a tight sweater or skirt on a day that's predicted to have a THI (Temperature and Humidity Index) of 88 — you'll really suffer as the clothes cut in at your waist, neck, and arms from a slight puffiness that may develop. Even an eighth of an inch of difference can be too much if the clothes are tight to begin with. During menstrual periods, women should wear looser-fitting clothes to reduce stress on abdomen, back, and breasts. Women who wear bras should wear a different size during their periods — or wear an adjustable bra.

Trying on Clothes

All clothing should allow the body to move freely. We've devised several easy body movements that can be helpful for people to determine the feel of clothes and whether or not they encumber or inhibit healthy activity.

Shirts and Blouses

You should be able to fit two fingers in at the collar and one finger in at the cuff of your shirts for maximum comfort. Sleeves should be long enough so elbows can bend freely without pulling at the shoulder and cuff (or tearing through the shirt!). When trying on shirts or blouses, lift your arms straight over your head. Do they move freely? Does the fabric fit well over the shoulders without tugging over the back and feeling as if it will rip? Lift your arms out at sides and twist from the waist. Does the shirt pull up from the pants or shirt? If it does it's too short. Does it pull tightly across the waist and sides? Cross your arms on your chest with elbows touching. Does the shirt fit across the back? Does it feel as if it's going to rip at the arm holes? If so it's too tight. Clasp your hands behind back and lift. Does the shirt or blouse pull tightly across the chest? How do the armholes feel? If there is a pull, arms are restricted in motion and the shirt or blouse could rip.

These same movements are helpful in choosing dresses, jackets, and coats. You should also wear a sweater underneath outer wear to get an idea of how it will feel in actual wearing conditions.

Pants and Trousers

You should be able to fit two fingers in at the waistband to allow for breathing. (Fingers should fit without your having to suck in your breath.) The fasteners should not pull tightly across the abdomen or make the pants too tight in the crotch or across the buttocks. Thigh muscles should have room to flex in the upper legs. If your thigh's circumference is sixteen inches, you really can't fit into fourteen-inch leg openings without seriously constricting muscle movement and circulation and without marking your legs.

When trying on pants and trousers, lift your arms out at sides and twist your body to the right and left. Does the waistline feel comfortable or does it cut into skin? Stand in a relaxed position and breathe normally. Does your abdomen move freely? Can you stand erect or are you forced into an uncomfortable posture by the tightness of the fasteners or fabric? Lift your arms out at your sides and bend first to the right and then to the left. Does the fabric cut into your flesh in any area? Does the material irritate any part of your legs or body? Does the fabric tug or pull at the crotch?

Stand and raise each leg out to the side. Does the fabric pull at the crotch or pull too tightly across the outer upper thigh? Stand straight, bend your leg at the knee and lift. Again, does the fabric pull or bind at any body area making it feel uncomfortable? Stand straight with your hands on your hips and do deep-knee bends. Check for pulling, tightness, chafing, and inhibition of movement. Walk around in the pants or trousers. Do your legs move well? Does the fabric rub or chafe between the legs or in the crotch? Is stride inhibited or movement uncomfortable?

Sit in front of a mirror. Are you comfortable? Do the pants pull at the knee or the crotch? Does the waistband cut in at the waist or the back? Can you breathe? Is there pressure on the abdomen? Are the thigh muscles able to flex? Stand up again and bend over at the waist. Does any part of the garment cut, bend, chafe, or pull? (Pay particular attention to the crotch area — too much pressure can harm delicate tissue or cause bladder irritations.) Straighten up again. Take a final look at yourself after these simple exertions. Do you look comfortable or strained? Has the fabric rubbed or marked the skin at the waist? After removing the garment check for telltale red seam marks in the thighs. If there are marks, the pants are too tight.

Skirts

Buttons, various fasteners, and zippers should not pull tightly across the abdomen or the buttocks. When trying on skirts (and dresses), stand straight and view the full body in a mirror. Does the fabric strain across abdomen at the hips or thighs? Stand straight with your hands on your hips and turn to each side. Does the skirt chafe at the waistband or pull the shirt or blouse too tightly? Using a mirror check the back of the skirt. Does it pull across the buttocks or the backs of the thighs? Walk at a normal pace in the skirt. Can you take an adequate stride, or are you hampered by tightness (especially at the knees)? Does the skirt ride up? (If it does it is too tight over the thighs.) Sit in front of a mirror. Are you comfortable? Does the fabric bind at the waist or pull tightly across the abdomen? Does the skirt ride up unbecomingly around the knees? (If so, the skirt is too tight.) Stand again and view your body. Do you look good — or rumpled? (If a new skirt looks rumpled when it's on your body, it doesn't fit you.) Has the fabric rubbed or chafed at the waist?

The best time to be critical about your wardrobe is before you buy it. Your own impression of how you look is the one that really matters; only you can know how you feel in clothes you wear. Any discomfort that manifests itself in the short period of time you try something on is an indication the garment is not for you. Wise shopping means buying and wearing clothes that are comfortable as well as well-priced for your budget. Truly good clothing buys meet the criterion of looking and feeling right for you. Good, healthy clothes needn't be expensive. Comparative shopping helps to keep clothing costs down. At the same time it helps insure you're getting the most healthful and comfortable clothes for your money.

Fig. 15–5. *A wool jersey jumpsuit gathered at the ankles with a tie has a loose, comfortably fitting V-neck top and push-up sleeves. The shoulders are cut wide for roominess and the suit can be worn over a t-shirt. The waist is loosely sashed with an obi. This suit can also be made in silk for a dressier look.*

The First Steps

Choose natural fibers as often as possible, particularly for garments that come in close contact with your skin. Dress comfortably when you shop for clothes and try to shop when you are in a good mood so you can give attention to your wardrobe and not your problems. Shopping while tense, anxious, or angry could limit your attentiveness to your ability to make good choices. It may also cause you to buy clothes you don't want or need.

Always try your choices on and do the simple body movements we've described in front of mirrors so you get a good idea how they look and fit. Making sure you can move freely and feel well in the clothes before you buy them can insure you'll like what you bought and wear it often. Never buy a garment that doesn't fit with the thought you'll lose enough weight in a short period of time to wear it. Chances are you will be wasting your money. Comfortable clothes make a person look beautiful, and that's what being healthy is about.

Don't hesitate to have a particular garment you like tailored to fit you. Cultivating a relationship with a seamstress or tailor who understands your ideas about healthy, comfortable dressing can be a good idea for developing a healthy wardrobe.

Dress for health clothes follow simple concepts that can be easily adapted to daily living. With a bit of ingenuity and some careful clothing selections just about anyone can begin dressing healthily and looking great. Dressing for health starts with a person's mental outlook and sense of individuality and encompasses attitudes about one's whole life style and experience.

Unfortunately most of the designs that are popularized in our culture are those that restrict and hamper the body, forcing its form into unnatural, ungraceful, and uncomfortable lines. The design of fabrics and clothes has always been used to define, either through acceptance or protest, the ideas of the age. It is as if culture is described by the garments worn. Much of the clothing worn by western civilizations has had the added strictures of ascribing morality and modesty to these designs. For example, if viewing female breasts is considered scandalous by a society, the breasts must be covered by cloth. However, this covering may serve two functions: it may sufficiently cover them to prevent others from seeing the bosom exists, or, perversely, it may, by the very act of covering them with sheer, diaphanous, or tight materials, emphasize and enhance the covered anatomy. The adage, "The more concealing, the more revealing," has this idea in mind.

Clothing designs rarely consider the health of the individual. If breasts must be covered to prevent lascivious eyes from peering at the flesh, heavy, encumbering fabrics can be used to make the whole body appear bulky and without much distinct form. These fabrics are at best uncomfortable, and at worst unwearable, because they hamper movement, are too warm for most climates, and prevent the wearer from doing little else than praying or sitting still. These have been good garments for imprisoning women under the guise of protecting their bodies from immoral wandering eyes. On the other hand, the equipment and virtual machinery that has gone into revealing the breasts has been just as unhealthy. Push-up pads, underwire cups, corsets, dipping necklines constrict the body to another type of immobility — one which places a woman and her breasts on display while hampering her movements, breathing, and circulation.

During some periods of history, cultural mores have concluded that other parts of the body are also too provocative to be viewed. The legs and bottom have born the brunt of these decisions with designs that have included pants, skirts, hoops, pantaloons, shorts, hose, and boots. Hemlines may rise, but so too must boot heights to compensate for the expanse of leg shown. These tightly-laced leathers may totally obstruct circulation and leave unsightly and dangerous dents, which often bruise the skin of the calves and shins. For hundreds of years, fashion has seen skirt lengths rise and plummet for no reason other than sexual titillation.

In the *The Unfashionable Human Body,* Bernard Rudofsky, an authority on the morality of dress, claims

> when the (shod) foot came out of hiding, its display may have shaken the moral foundation of many a strong man. But no sooner had he regained

his composure than he began to prospect for neighboring territories. To keep him on the right track, and let him savor his discoveries, the hitherto secret regions from ankle to thigh had to be declassified one by one . . . . Unavoidably though, when thighs lose their appeal as plat du jour, the curtain has to come down on legs all the way. To recharge them with eroticism, hemlines must forever rise and fall. (p. 62)

In many respects we have become enslaved by fashion, wearing clothes that shackle us and endanger our health in the process. Slacks and pants, once thought to be great liberators, particularly for women, have taken on the characteristics of torture-chamber implements in the form of designer jeans. Here the selling point emphasis is on their tightness! They are constructed to hug the body in the culturally desirable right places and, like tightly laced boots, leave the tattoo marks of seams and thread embedded in the thighs and provide a breeding ground for bacterial growth in the crotch and a tourniquet effect on the abdomen. Because wearing them insures social desirability for men and women alike, potential buyers are intimidated into slimming themselves with the pertinacity of anorexics. Skinny, life-starving fashions, and skinny, body-starving diets go hand in hand in our society.

Each part of the human form has been subjected to fashion-design attention, either to mask or heighten its potential for voyeuristic excitation. The waist and abdomen of both men and women have been the focus of some of the worst antihealth contraptions ever invented, including the corset and girdle. These viselike implements are not relegated merely to history books. Some very modern fashions require the wearer to don them in modified and sleek forms as underclothes to smooth out "lumps and bumps" under thin fabrics. Some of these garments are called Control Top panties, Slimliners, and one is cleverly called, The I Can't Believe It's a Girdle, Girdle because it is allegedly too comfortable to be so cleverly slimming!

The corset was considered by some to be an instrument of mutilation for the purpose of lowering the subject's vitality and rendering her personally and obviously unfit for work. This was desirable perhaps in a civilization content with slavery, but corseting hardly fits in the 1980s when women as well as men are free to work and lead active lives. Admittedly, modern women do not wear whalebone corsets that dislocate their bones and displace organs, but fashion still insists on revamping the natural lines of the body to conform to style with bizarre clothes and underwear. This new underwear, which is guaranteed to produce sexual allure, nips in the waist, crushes the ribs and belly to make it smooth and flat, and uplifts the breasts in much the same way the nineteenth century garments crippled their wearers.

Fashion-design vanity has also attacked the modern male of the species offering him, too, the clean and unbumpy lines produced by tight, stretch undershirts and shorts. Some men's undershorts have been architecturally designed to resculpt the shape of the buttocks, offering the male rear the dubious role of sex object, similar to women's breasts. Men wear skinny jeans and body shirts as much as women do. To fit them, both actually and figuratively, they must slim themselves as well.

Environmentally aware individuals wouldn't dream of wearing clothes made from endangered species of animals and mammals. But creating synthetic replacements for whalebone can be just as environmentally pernicious. Natural dressers wishing to dress low on the technology chain will find that simple clothing designs are much more suited to this aim than are the synthetic foundations and fashions found in today's super-styled marketplace.

The ancients, with their cloth-draped bodies had a far healthier impression of what dress should be. They were more interested in the personal style imparted on clothes by an individual than the interest vested by moderns in conformity and uniformity of design. Fashion designs that display a person's innate qualities rather than those qualified and quantified by the society-at-large are more healthy in that they allow a person to display ingenuity, wit, integrity, and style rather than parrot the dictates of trendsetters and profit makers who are more interested in their balance sheets than their customers' well-being.

Perhaps if in our efforts to dress healthily, we adapt some of the ideas of the ancients, coupled with a common-sense attitude about the lines and forms of our own bodies and an awareness as environmental needs, we will develop fashion designs that enhance health rather than destroy it.

16

The whole story

For the past two hundred years society has plunged ahead creating a world of highly sophisticated and advanced technology, all in the interest of conquering nature and creating better living conditions. But unfortunately, this thrust has severely burdened the earth's natural resources, polluted its atmosphere, and, in many ways, virtually imperiled life on the planet. It has created an ultimate paradox: an automated, technologically controlled world, where machines do the work, but no one can benefit from the labor-saving devices because no living creature can survive in the polluted environment. For fleeting moments our scientific advancements bring great progressive and innovative changes. But over the long haul, these have proven to be extremely costly to the environment, and they will continue to be, unless the methods of production are drastically changed.

This is evident in the shift from natural-fiber production to synthetic-fiber production, which has intensified stress on the environment over the last thirty-five years. The energy to produce natural fibers comes from a renewable source: the sun. Animals and plants produce fibers in a natural environment — without producing noxious wastes. Synthetics, on the other hand, require two sources of energy for their production: fossil fuels (petroleum and gases) are the raw material of synthetics and additional energy (often fossil fuels) act as catalysts to transform the raw materials into fiber. Synthetic-fiber production uses up nonrenewable energy sources, a process that is ecologically wasteful and causes chemical waste, air, and water pollution, a process that is ecologically dangerous. These processes involve the first part of a garment's life.

During later stages in the life of synthetics, wear and care of the fabrics require additional energy use and cause more environmental abuse. Natural fibers may be cleaned with natural soaps, steam, and washing sodas. Synthetics, on the other hand, require strong detergents, water softeners, toxic cleaning solvents, and substances that are caustic to the skin and hazardous to the ecosystem.

In the final stages of a garment's life, disposal becomes part of the picture. Natural fibers are a part of the ecosystem and don't accumulate as wastes. When returned to the earth, natural fibers are broken down by bacterial enzymes. Synthetic fibers have no natural enzymatic antagonists to degrade them after disposal. They must be destroyed by burning, which releases toxic fumes and pollutes the air, or they accumulate as waste. Synthetic fabrics do not degrade, they last forever. Longevity in a fabric is desirable; interminableness is not.

It seems that all arguments eventually lead to economics and costs. The price for damaging the environment enters many realms — perhaps the most costly of which is social. Polluted air and water can irrevocably harm the ecosystem and ultimately poison all life on the planet. The consumer is the one who pays for these problems, first suffering the injury to health that occurs from a fouled environment and then suffering the insult of paying, through hidden costs, the taxes and fines for pollution that are levied by government on manufacturers.

Another aspect of this argument is conservation. Saving energy is different from not using up resources, and conserving is something that each little person can do to make a big contribution to solving the problem. Each of us can use less of things, but each of us can make more out of what we already have by using simple principles in which clothing can play a large role. Some of the environmental problems of the modern world have made many of us feel deprived not just of material things but of emotional and sensory communication. However, healthy clothes can make living easier by enhancing our bodies' thermostatic controls and basic environmental design and by helping us maintain a balanced interaction with the environment and others around us.

Conserving the body's energy as well as the energy of the environment may be achieved simultaneously by wearing ecologically sound, natural garments that suit climatic conditions. The body may be viewed as a mini-solar collector, a device that stores energy from the sun; wearing proper clothing can enhance the body's capabilities for storing and releasing energy when needed. This is particularly important today in view of the federally enforced temperature controls which mandate an indoor temperature range of sixty-five degrees in winter and eighty degrees in summer. The body's normal "comfort zone" rests in an area between seventy-four degrees and seventy-eight degrees; one of the ways to achieve these temperatures in a closed environment such as a home or office is by regulating the types and amounts of clothing worn.

Simple energy conservation can be achieved by adding or removing clothes. But more efficiency can be added to this by wearing energy-efficient fibers, those that retain heat in cold weather and absorb moisture and allow perspiration to evaporate in warm weather. Wool, linen, cotton, and silk are fibers with multiple energy-efficiency. They don't pollute or overexpend energy in their production, care, or disposal, and they provide the most comfortable and healthful bodily environments possible. Wearing clothes made with these natural fibers can help the body stabilize itself in the comfort zone.

Since body temperature is so important to comfort, researchers have devised insulation values to compare various types of clothes; the term "clo" is used as the unit of measure on a clothing thermal-value scale. A value of 1 has been applied to a men's business suit, and fractional values are applied to other articles of clothing in the wardrobe. Clo values have been determined for most clothes, and we recommend the clothing industry tag garments with them as a helpful guide for consumers to determine efficient wear.

Healthy bodies burn food as fuel to generate and regulate heat and to provide energy to perform life's tasks. In a variation of the life-cycle theme, healthy clothes can conserve this energy and preserve the health of the body to start the process over again.

Our economic system survives on profit, and there is fear that anything that interferes with progress, a proponent of profit, is dangerous to it. Technology is viewed as essential for continued successful survival. Perhaps there is also some fear that if consumers become conscious of the impact their clothes have on the environment as well as how they affect health, in the way they've become conscious about their food, they'll demand cessation of clothing production or stop wearing clothes altogether. Obviously, the food industry didn't collapse as soon as people became more aware of nutrition. On the contrary, the exposure of deficiencies in diets has prompted many food manufacturers to produce better-quality foods, and spurred the development of many new, alternative, and profitable food enterprises.

There's tremendous profit potential in environmentally sound endeavors, particularly when it comes to clothes. We are not only what we eat; we are what we wear! Perhaps the development of a revolutionized clothes consciousness would mean new improvements in clothing manufacturing and technology. A whole new alternative style of dressing could develop centered around "health cloth" stores and better-quality, hand-made garments.

Just as many people have gone "back to the land" to produce their own food, many will go "back to the loom" to produce their own clothes. This alternative need not depress the clothing industry. Rather, it could prod it on to vie with individuals in terms of quality production, rather than the quantity-production syndrome that seems to rule the present system.

Essentially, the basic economy to be considered should be the cost to human lives and health. Only we can control our environment, and only we can change a system currently based on the economy of dollars to one that's based on an economy of health. Dressing for health can contribute greatly to preserving natural resources. We can create our own individual energy conservation by the clothes we wear and at the same time create heightened sensory awareness in fashions that let us breathe, touch, relate, and live in harmony with our world.

Resources for the natural dresser

Clothing

Ahimsa Imports
9 Creek Lane
Mill Valley, CA 94941
(415) 383–4990
Natural-fiber clothing

Alaya
848 Cole St.
San Francisco, CA 94117
Natural-fiber clothes

Ananda
Box 805
Monroe, NY 10950
(914) 782–5575
Cotton traditional yoga clothes

Antartex Sheepskin Shops
P.O. Box No. 1
New Lebanon, NY 12125
(800) 621–5199

Brooks Brothers
346 Madison Ave.
New York, NY 10017
Men's and women's fine cotton
    shirts and blouses, wool
    clothing

Canal Jean
504 Broadway
New York, NY
(212) 431–4765
All natural-fiber clothing

Deva
Route 8, Hwy 40 West,
Dept. e
Frederick, MD 21701
(301) 662–2644
Natural clothing, cotton draw-
    string pants

Dharmacrafts
Cambridge Zen Center
263 North Harvard Street
Allston, MA 02134
Natural-fiber pants and skirts

diddingtons ltd.
143 Prince St.
New York, NY 10012
(212) 228–1748
All-natural clothes

Govinda
340 W. 55 St.
New York, NY 10019
(212) 765–9690
All-natural clothing, including
   outer garments

Kimono-tique
475 Broome St.
New York, NY 10013
(212) 226–5532
Kimonos

Kreeger and Son, Ltd.
16 West 46
New York, NY 10017
(212) 575–7825
Camping gear and natural-fiber
   clothes

L. L. Bean
863 Casco St.
Freeport, ME 04033
Camping gear and natural-fiber
   clothes

Landau
114 Nassau St.
Princeton, NJ 08540
All-wool ponchos

Lynn Dougherty
376 Broome St.
New York, NY 10013
(212) 966–9707
Designer clothes

Material Plane
1320 Pearl St.
Boulder, CO 80302
Cotton, traditional folk and yoga
   clothes

Maltby-Gillies
38 Chauncy St.
Suite 408-N
Boston, MA 02111
Fine cotton clothes

Miso
416 West Broadway
New York, NY 10012
(212) 226–4955

Nandi Imports
P. O. Box 546
Mill Valley, CA 94941
(415) 388–1660
Shirts, pants

Norm Thompson Outfitters, Inc.
13700 NW Science Park Drive
Portland, OR 97229
(503) 644–2666
Natural-fiber clothes

Patti Howard
Dept. WD9
322 Main St.
Stamford, CT 06901
Women's cotton t-shirts

Putumayo
857 Lexington Ave.
New York, NY 10021
(212) 734–3111
Pants, dresses, ponchos, accessories

Sam's Shod
P. O. Box 398
Taos, NM 87571
(505) 758–4496
Dresses

Solviva
P. O. Box 1263
Ogunquit, ME 03907
Natural clothes, women's ac-
cessories (including menstrual
sponges)

Tamala Design with Bagel
155 Prince St.
New York, NY 10012
(212) 473–0197
Natural clothing

Three Wishes
355 Broadway
New York, NY 10013
(212) 925–1065
Pants, shirts, jackets

Undercovers
Box 1674
Old Sudbury Rd.
Lincoln, MA 01773
Women's cotton slips

Water Witch
Main Street — A
Castine, ME 04421
Fine cotton clothing

Clothing: Mail-Order Only

Astral Enterprises
P. O. Box 70190
Seattle, WA 98107
Wool clothes

Cable Car Clothiers
Robert Kirk, Ltd.
No. 150, Post St.
San Francisco, CA 94108
(415) 397–7733
Some natural-fiber selections

Christananda
977 Ashbury St.
San Jose, CA 95126
(408) 292–6359
Cotton drawstring pants, shorts,
skirts

Coming Attractions
1524 Springhill Road
McLean, VA 22102
Natural-fiber clothes

David Morgan
Box 70190
Seattle, WA 98107
(206) 282–3300
Welsh fisherman's smocks—
all wool

Especially Maine
Rt. 1, Dept. CJ8
Arundel, ME 04046
Cotton and wool clothes

Folkwear
Box 98
Forestville, CA 95436

Garnet Hills
358 B Main St.
Franconia, NH 03580
Cotton shirts, wool underwear

Gokeys
84 S. Wabaha Street
Saint Paul, MN 55107
(612) 293–3911

Good Things Collective
245 Main St.
Northampton, MA 01060
(413) 586–6590
100 percent natural-fiber clothing
and natural-style shoes

Intuition Enterprises
3213 Longfellow
So. Minneapolis, MN 55407
Hand-dyed 100 percent cotton
stockings

J. Jill Ltd.
Dept. N924 Stockbridge Rd.
Great Barrington, MA 01230
Cotton dresses and cotton-flannel
blouses

Joetta Lawrence
520 Maxwell
Boulder, CO 80302
Natural-fiber clothes

Land's End
2317 N. Elston Ave.
Chicago, IL 60614
Cotton and wool sport clothes

Natural Fiber Stockings
P. O. Box 239
Menlo Park, CA 94025
Cotton and silk-fiber stockings

Talbots
Dept. FD
Higham, MA 02043
Some all-natural fiber selections
in men's and women's clothing

Unique Clothing Warehouse
718 Broadway
New York, NY
(212) 674–1767
Some seleccted all-natural fiber
clothing

Children's Clothing

The Chocolate Soup
249 East 77
New York, NY 10021
(212) 861–2210

Little Bits
1036 Third
New York, NY
(212) 838–5964

Small Business
101 Wooster St.
New York, NY
(212) 966–1425

Fabrics

Carol Brown
Putney, VT 05346
Natural fabrics

Fabrication
146 E. 56 St.
New York, NY 10022
Natural fibers

Mail-Order Only

Natural Fiber Fabric Club
Dept. VP12
521 Fifth Ave.
New York, NY 10017
Natural fabrics

Thai Silk Co.
9 Suriwongse Road
Box 906 6PO
Bangkok, Thailand
Handwoven silk

Yarns:

Mail-Order Only

Harrisville Design
Harrisville, NH 03450
Natural-fiber yarns

Minaki Trading Co.
Minaki, Ontario
POX 1JO Canada
Undyed wool yarn

Patterns

International Printworks Inc.
110 Gould Street
Needham, MA 02194
Wrap and tie skirts

Shoes

Birkenstock
1320 Pearl St.
Boulder, CO 80302

Cordwainer Creations
Wild Orchard Farms
Deerfield, NH 03037

Foot Naturals
446 Union Ave.
Paterson, NJ 07522
(201) 942–4444

Impressionistic
462 Ave of the Americas
New York, NY 10011
(212) 243–7918

Shakti Corporation
3401 K St., N.W.
Washington, DC 20007
(202) 338–9338

Mail-Order Only

Terrapin Trading Co.
Box 217
Somerville, MA 02143
Cotton shoes

Selected
bibliography

Balletine, Rudolph. 1978. *Diet and Nutrition: A Holistic Approach*. Honesdale, PA: The Himalayan International Institute.

_____, ed. 1977. *The Science of Breath*. Glenview, IL: The Himalayan International Institute.

Benjamin, Ben E. 1978. *Are You Tense?* New York: Pantheon Books.

Bergler, Edmund. 1953. *Fashion and the Unconscious*. New York: Robert Brunner.

Birren, Faber. 1978. *Color Psychology and Color Therapy*. Secaucus, NJ: The Citadel Press.

Boucher, Francois. (n.d.) *20,000 Years of Fashion: A History of Costume and Personal Adornment*. New York: Harry N. Abrams.

Cannon, Walter B. 1967. *The Wisdom of the Body.* New York: Norton.

Commoner, Barry. 1974. *The Closing Circle: Nature, Man and Technology*. New York: Bantam.

_____. 1976. *The Poverty of Power*. New York: Knopf.

Corbman, Bernard P. 1975. *Textiles: Fiber to Fabric*. New York: McGraw-Hill.

Debakey, Michael; and Grotto, Antonio. 1977. *The Living Heart*. New York: David McKay.

Fast, Julius. 1971. *You and Your Feet*. New York: St. Martins Press.

Flugel, J. C. 1966. *The Psychology of Clothes*. London: Hogarth Press.

Fourt, L.; and Hollies, N. 1970. *Clothing: Comfort and Function*. New York: Marcel Dekker.

Fuller, R. Buckminster. 1969. *Operating Manual for Spaceship Earth*. New York: Simon and Schuster.

Gernsheim, Alison. (n.d.). *Fashion and Reality: 1840–1914*. London: Faber and Faber.

Graham, F. Lanier. 1979. *The Rainbow Book*. Rev. ed. San Francisco: Vintage Books.

Hollen, Norma; and Saddler, Jane. 1973. *Textiles*. New York: MacMillan.

Horn, Marilyn J. 1975. *The Second Skin*. Boston: Houghton Mifflin.

Mann, Felix. 1971. *Acupuncture: The Ancient Chinese Art of Healing and How It Works Scientifically*. New York: Vintage Books.

Masunaga, Shizuto. 1977. *Zen Shiatsu*. Tokyo: Japan Publications.

Mead, Margaret. 1970. *Male and Female*. New York: William Morrow.

Montagu, Ashley. 1978. *Touching: The Human Significance of Skin*. 2d. ed. New York: Harper and Row.

Ohashi, Wataru. 1976. *Do-It-Yourself Shiatsu*. New York: E. P. Dutton.

Ott, John. 1977. *Health and Light*. New York: Pocket Books.

Rudofsky, Bernard. 1971. *The Unfashionable Human Body*. New York: Doubleday.

Samuels, Michael; and Bennet, Harold Zina. 1973. *The Well Body Book*. Berkeley, CA: The Book Works.

Stobaugh, Robert; and Yergin, Daniel, eds. 1979. *Energy Future*. New York: Random House.

Strobbe, Maurice A. 1971. *Understanding Environmental Pollution*. St. Louis, MO: C. V. Mosby Co.

Todd, Mabel Elsworth. 1978. *The Thinking Body*. Brooklyn, NY: Dance Horizons.

Windgate, Isabel B. 1976. *Textile Fabrics and Their Selection*. Englewood Cliffs, NJ: Prentice-Hall.

Index

AATCC (American Association of Textile Chemists and Colorists), 183
AATT (Association for Textile Technology), 183
Abbayah, 105, 129
Abdomen, 80, 133
Absorption of chemicals, 41
Acceptable Concentration Standards, 36
Achilles tendon, 92
Acids, allergies to, 38
Acrilan, 51
Acrylics, 51–54
Acupuncture, 98, 100
Algae in water systems, 180
Agate, 121
Alexander the Great, 69
A-line dresses
    for kids, 150
    for women, 161
Allergens, 35, 38. See also Dyes, as allergens, 35, 38
Alpaca, 72, 74
American Standards Association, 36
Ames, Bruce, 41
Ancient civilizations, clothing
    concepts of, 114. See also Clothing
Angora, 72, 74
Animal hair, 137
    fibers, 72–74
Anorexic, 203
Antaeus, Greek warrior, 98
Appliqué, 153
Aquarius, 127
Arabs, 129
Architecture of body, 84, 111
Aries, 126, 127
Arteriosclerosis, 93
Asanas, 186
Ashram, 186
ASTM (American Society for Testing Materials), 183

Avlin, 50. See also Polyesters
Azoic dyes, 43
Aztecs, 122

Back to the land, 209
Back to the loom, 209
Bacteria, resistance in linen to, 65
Ballentine, Rudolph, 79–80
Basic dyes, 43
Belgium and flax production, 64
Bell, Quintin, 17
Belts and kids' clothes, 153
Benjamin, Ben, 85
Benzene, 180
Berber trousers, 130
Beryl, 121
Biodegradability of detergents and soaps, 180
Birkenstock Shoe Company, 95, 158
Black and absence of light, 123
Bladder, irritations from tight clothing, 199. See also Genitourinary system
Blankets, 186–187
    and children, 143
Bleach, 180–181
Blends (of fibers)
    durability, 149
    in suits, 161
Bleut, 21
Bloomer, Amelia Jenks, 31
Bloomers, 31
Blouses, 161
    choosing proper size of, 197
Blum, Arlene, 41
Body consciousness, 111, 150, 159
Body size
    changes in, 113
    expansion in heat of, 197
Body suits, 149

Bombyx mori, 67
Boots, 95
  canvas, 95
  fleece-lined, 154
  leather, 95, 154
  plastic, 95
  vinyl, 95
Braiding, 118
Bras and menstrual periods, 197
Brassieres and stress on breathing, 80
Breathing, 78, 79, 202
Bunions, 93–94
Burnoose, 129
Bursas, 93. See also bunions
Bustle, 24, 29
Byzantium and silk production, 66

Caftan, 18, 129, 173, 188
Calluses, 93
Camel hair, 72, 73
Camisole, 173
Camouflage, 116
Cancer, 127
Cannon, Walter, MD, 103
Capricorn, 127
Carcinogens, 35, 41, 42, 56
Cartilage, 86
Cashmere, 72, 73
Caustic sodas and rayon production, 75
Chemical additives, 35–36, 39–42
Childbirth and color, 121
Children's clothes. See also Comfort; Cleanliness;
    Durability; Sweaters
  and helpful hints for choosing, 157
  and labels, 185
  and protection, 144, 153
Chroma, 124
  and personality and flair, 124
Chromopathy, 122
Circulation, 81–83
  hampering of, 202
Cleanliness, 143
  and children's development, 150
  and dress-up clothes for kids, 150
Climates, clothing for all, 103–106
Clo and thermal value of clothes, 208
Clothes consciousness, revolution in, 209
Clothes, trying on, 197–199
Clothing
  appliquéd and embroidered, 153
  and comfort, 201
  and confidence, 191
  and conformity, 193
  and flexibility, 193
  Greek, 20
  as indicators of status, 27–28
  and intimidation, 193
  and menstrual periods, 197
  Middle East, 20
  in the 1960s, 29–30
  and personal needs, 195
  in Pleistocene era, 17–18
  and relief of tension, 193
  Renaissance, 22, 29
  Roman, 20
  and sense of security, 193
  as status symbol, 24
  and the weather, 195
Clothing styles, differentiated for men and women,
    28–29
Codpiece, 29

Colon, 83
Color, 121–128. See also Harmony; Intensity of color;
    Primary color systems; Secondary color systems
  coordination and harmonies, 125
  and evil spirits, ill health, 121
  and fashion consciousness, 122
  in healing and therapy, 121
  and psychological factors, 124
  and social messages, 122
  spiritual aspects of, 126
Color wheel, 123
Combing, 65
Comfort, 143
  and children's clothes, 149, 150
  and children's development, 143
  and children's shoes, 144
Comfort zone, 208
Committee 17, 35
Comparisons of Natural and Man-Made Fibers (chart),
    76–77
Conservation, 159, 207, 210
Control Top panties, 203
Consumer Products Safety Commission, 40, 146
Consumer Reports, 184
Corduroy, 146
  for children, 146
  coveralls, 150
Coronary thrombosis, 82
Corsets, 24–25, 30, 203, 204
Cotton, 61–64, 143
  canvas, 153
  canvas shoes, 156
  care of, 63, 64
  characteristics of, 61, 62–63
  denim, 153
  diapers, 153
  in India, Africa, Americas, 61
  in natural dresser's wardrobe, 159
  production of, 61
  recommended for children, 143
  texture, 118
Cordwainer Creations, 95
Corns, 93
Coveralls, 133, 153
  for summer and warmth, 154
Covers. See also Blankets
  for children, 143
  as protection from sun, 153
Creativity
  and dress, 109–110
  and self-expression, 114
Creslan, 52
Cystitis, 84

Dacron, 50
de Bakey, Michael, 81
de Chardonnet and silk creation, 75
Delaney Amendment, 36
Denim, 146
  for children, 146
  cotton, brushed, 150
Denim weave, 119
Depression. See Respiration
Dermatitis, 35, 42, 43
  and dyes, 84
Design, 116
Detergents, 180
Dhoti, 18
Diabetes and shoes, 93
Diapers, 144
Diaphragm, 80, 133

Digestion, 83
Direct dyes, 43, 44
Disperse dyes, 43–44
Djarellaba, 129
Dobby, 119
Dorsal canal. See Skeletal System
Dow Chemical Company, 52
Drapery of clothing, 111–115
Drawstrings
    and kids' clothes, 149
    and pants, 130, 159
    and shorts, 133
    and skirts, 133
    and sweatpants, 150
Dress codes, 187
Dress for health
    adapting to, 187
    concepts of, 201
    mental outlook and, 201
    and bodily functions, 79
Dry cleaning. See Labels
Du Pont, 48, 50, 51, 54
Durability
    and kids clothes, 144, 146
    and blends, 149
    of fabrics, 150
    patches to provide for, 153
Dyes, 43–46, 143
    as allergens, 43, 44
    allergies to, 38
    as carcinogens, 43
    infant responses to absorption, 45
    labels, 182
    lack of necessity and kids, 153
Dynel, 53

Edema, 82
    and improperly fitted shoes, 93
Effect of chemicals, 36–38.
    See also Synthetics; Synthetic fibers
Egyptians, 129, 133
    and fabric cleaning, 179
Elastic, avoidance of, 149
Elbows. See Points of support
Embroidery, 130, 133, 153
Emeralds, 121
Emergency Treatment and Medicine, 45
Emotions, expression of, 101
Energy conservation and clothing, 191
Energy efficient fibers, 208
Energy flow. See Meridians
Enka. See polyesters
Environment, clothing design and, 159
Environmental design of body, 208
Environmental impact, 185, 206
    of chemical additives, 42–43
    concern for hazards, 110
    and contaminants, 104
    of dyes, 45–46
    of natural fiber products, 58
    stress and detergent production, 180
    of synthetic fiber production, 56–57
    and temperature, 104
Environmental Mutagenic Society, 35, 36
Enzymatic antagonists and synthetic fibers, 207
Equilibrium. See Homeostasis
Etruscans, 129
Exposure to cold and wet climate and sickness, 154
Eye diseases and color, 121

Fabric care. See Labels

Fasteners, 146
    stringties, 149
    zippers, 149
Federal Trade Commission, 181
Feet, 89–96
    eroticization of, 91
    and healthy development in children, 144, 156, 158
Felting, 118
Fiber reactive dyes, 44
Finishing, 143
Flame resistance standards, 146
Flame retardants, 40–43, 143
    allergies to, 38
Flannel and warmth, 63
Flax. See Linen
Flammable Fabrics Act (1953), 146
Flugel, Dr. J. C., 29
Footwear complementary to body, 89–90. See also Shoes
Form, volume and space, 116
Fossil fuels and synthetic production, 207
Freedom of movement, 188
Fuller, Buckminster, 34
Fur Products Labeling Act, 183

Gastrointestinal tract, 83
Genitourinary system, 83–84
Germs, breeding ground and, 153
Gabardine, 119
Gemini, 127
Gold, Marian, 41
Good Housekeeping, 184
Gorro, Antonio, 81
Greeks, 129
Guatemalan, 137, 176

Hackling, 65
Hallmarks. See Labels
Hallux Valgus, 94
Hand, coarseness and rigidity and crispness and softness
    of, 118
Harem pants, 130, 173
Harmonies, color, 103, 125, 126
Harmony, 210
    and digestion, 83
Harvey, William, 81
Health cloth, 209
Hemlines, 202–203
Hemorrhaging and color, 121
Hemorrhoids, 82
Hermitage, 69
Himation, 114
Holistic health, 97
Homeostasis, 103–106
Hoods and body warmth, 144, 154
Houpelande, 21
Housing the body, 129
Hue, 123
    and combining, 125
Hulepa, 176
Hyperpigmentation, 43
Hypertension, 82
Hyperventilation. See Breathing

IFI (International Fabricare Institute), 183
Illium, 87
Ingestion of chemicals, 37
Ingrown toenails, 94
Inhalation of chemicals, 37
Intensity of color, 123
Interchangeable wardrobe, 190
Ironing. See Labels

Ischium, 87

Jackets, 134, 153, 190
  cardigan, 161
  down-filled, 154
  hand-dyed silk, 173
  quilted, 154
  unstructured, 161
  for women, 161
  wrap, 161
Jacquard and brocades, 119
Jade, 121
Jaundice and color cure, 121
Jeans, 119
  and comfort, 203
Jersey, wool, 172
Jumpers, 150
Jupiter, 127
Justinian, 67

Karate suit, 161
  wrap jacket and, 161
  drawstring pants and, 161
Khaki, 119
Kilt, 133
Kimonos, 18
  for children, 143, 146, 172
  embroidered, 172
  at home and evening wear, 172
  silk, 172
Knees. See Points of support
Knitting, 118, 120
Kodel. See Polyesters
Kurta, 130

Labels, 179–185
  and clothing selection, 179
  limitations of, 182
Lactic acid, 85
Lapis lazuli, 121
Layering, 188, 190
  for outdoor wear and children, 144, 146
  indoors, 161
  for warmth, 105, 106, 113, 159, 161
LDs (Median Lethal Doses), 36
Leather boots, 154
Ligaments, 90
Leno, 119
Leo, 127
Libra, 127
Life cycles, 101–103
Light, 117
Line, 116
Linen, 64–66, 143
  care of, 65–66
  characteristics of, 65–66
  Egyptian, 19
  and natural dresser's wardrobe, 159
  production of, 64–65, 66
  texture of, 118
Little Dressing, 139–158
Lunar cycle and control of tides, 101
Lycra. See Spandex

Man-made fibers, 146. See also Synthetic fiber;
    Synthetics comparison with natural fibers, 35,
    48, 57, 76–77 (chart)
Mantle, 114
Mars, 127
Marvess. See Olefins
Menstrual cycle, 101

Mercerization, 63, 183
Mercury, 127
Meridians, 97, 98
Merino wool, 69, 70. See also Wool
Middle East, 129
Mini-solar collector, 208
Mittens, 144
Modacrylic, 53
Mohair, 72, 73
Montagu, Ashley, 140
Moon, 127
Moors, 129
Mores, 202
Morocco, 129
Mother Earth, 98
Movement, inhibition in children, 143
Mordant dyes, 44
Mulberry trees, 67
Muscles, 85
Muscular tension, 84
  effects on breathing and circulation, 85
Mutagens, 35

Native Americans, 122
Natural dresser, 109–115, 130, 133, 159, 176, 181, 193,
    204
  and rayon, 76
Natural fibers, 58–77, 106, 191
  and bacteria, 84
  brushed, 153
  care of, 59
  in children's clothes, 144
  choice of, 201
  choosing of, 181
  and comfort, 84
  comparison with man-made fibers, 35, 48, 57,
    76–77 (chart)
  cleaning and, 185
Natural resources
  use of, 110
  depletion of, 206–210
Nephritis, 82
Nerve paths, 110
Neuroma, 92
Newton, Sir Isaac, 122
Nightwear
  and comfort, 195
  and labels, 185
Nile River, 179
NIOSH (National Institute of Occupational Safety and
    Health, 36, 41
NIOSH Toxicological Studies, 37
NTA (nitrilotri-acetic acid) to replace phosphates, 181
Nutrition, 106
Nylon, 43, 48–50
  characteristics of, 49–50
  chemical additives, 50
  production of, 42

Obi, 130, 161
Ohashi, Wataru, 191
Olefins, 55–56
Oriental medicine, 98
Orlon, 51
OSHA (Occupational Safety and Health Administration,
    36
Overalls, 144, 146
  for adults, 133
  for children, 149
  dress-up, 150
Overcoats, 188

Oxygenation, 79

Pants
    Berber, 173
    choosing proper sizes, 198
    drawstring, 159, 173
    harem, 130, 173
    short, 153
Pallette, 125–126, 128
Palpitations and heat stress, 105
Parents Magazine, 184
Pelvic girdle, 130
Pelvis, 87
Penis. *See* Genitourinary system
Peristalsis, 83
Perkins, William Henry, 41
Permanent Care Labeling Rule, 181
Perspiration, 84
Petrochemical industry, 26, 47, 180
Permeability of human scrotum, 37
Petroleum in detergents, 180
Phlebitis, 82
Phenol, 42
    and benzene, 180
    and toxicity, 180
Phosphates, 180
Pile, 119. *See also* Velvets; Velours
Pima cotton, 184
Pisces, 127
Plague, 121
Planetary cycles, 101
    and individuals, 101
    and the weather and seasons, 101
Plastics in diapers, 144
Play clothes, 150. *See also* Children's clothes
Points of support, 111–112
Pollution, 110, 206, 207. *See also* Synthetics
Polychlorinated biphenyls, 42–43
Polyesters, 39, 50–51
    characteristics of, 50–51
    production of, 50
Polypropelene fibers. *See* Olefins
Poncho, 105, 115, 137
Porosity, 65
Posture and shoes, 91–92
Postures. *See* Asanas
Poulaine, 91
Prana, the vital life force, 99
Prang color system, 123
Precious stones. *See* Color
Primary color systems, 123
Pubes, 87

Quality control, 184
Quilting, 137

Radiation, protection from sun's, 105
Ramie, 66
Rashes and wet clothes (kids), 153
The Rational Dress Society, 30–31
Rayon, 39, 75–76
Reflexology, 100
Respiration, 79–81
Retting, 64
Rheumatism and color, 122
Rippling, 64
Rolled sleeves, 190
Romans, 129
Rudofsky, Bernard, 202

Safety
    and the environment, 159
    regulations, 159
Sagittarius, 126, 127
Sandals, 90, 94–95, 156
Sanforization, 183
Sapphires, 121
Saran, 56
Sari, 18
Sarong, 172
Saturn, 127
Scarf, 154
    worn as a sash, 114
Scorpio, 126, 127
Scots, 133
Scutching, 64
Seamstress, 190
Secondary color systems, 123
Secondary support of abdomen and buttocks, 111–112
SEF Modacrylic, 53
Self-sufficiency lessons and clothes, 157
Semi-precious stones. *See* Color
Sensory awareness, 210
Serge, 119
Sericin, 67
Sexual
    cycles, 101
    stereotyping, 111
    titillation, 202
Shades, 123
Shakti Shoes, 95
Shawl, 115, 172
Shiatsu, 98, 100
Shirts, choosing proper sizes, 197
Shoes. *See also* Footwear; Posture and shoes; Sandals
    Birkenstocks, 95, 158
    canvas, 156
    and children, 144, 154
    comfort in, 187–188
    Cordwainer Creations, 95
    early shoes as sandals, 9
    importance of fit, 94, 96
    jogging, 156
    Shakti Shoes, 95
    sneakers, 156
Shorts, 133
Shoulders, 86, 133
    for dress support, 161
    points of support and children, 149
Si Ling Chi, 66
Silk, 19, 22, 65–66
    care of, 68–69
    characteristics of, 68
    elasticity of, 68
    and natural dresser's wardrobe, 159
    production of, 58, 66–69
    texture and comfort, 118
Skeletal system, 86–88
Skin, 139
    absorption of chemicals, 37, 84
    protection from sun and cancer, 153
Skirts, choosing proper sizes, 199
Sleepers for children, 143, 146
Sleeping cycle patterns, 102
Sleepwear for comfort, 103
Slimliners, 203
Smock, bat-wing, 173
Soaking, 64, 180
Soap and biodegradability, 180
Solar cycle, 101
Solvents, allergies to, 38

Soviet Union and flax production, 64
Spandex, 54
Spectrum, colors in, 122
Spine, 86
Stability. *See* Homeostasis
Standardized fabric qualities. *See* Labels
Standardized flammability test, 146
Sternum, 86
Stress and bodily reactions, 79
Strokes, 82
Success orientation and clothes, 161
Suits, men, 25, 30
Sun and renewable energy, 127, 206
Sundress, 161
Support hose and circulation restrictions, 188
Surah, 119
Suspenders, 153, 161
Sweat, 104, 105
Sweaters, 143, 150
    for children, 143, 150
    hand-knitted, 173
Sweatshirt, 133
Sweatsuits, 150
Swimsuits
    wet, 153
    for kids, 153
Synthetic fiber, 206, 207
    and children's clothing, 143
    comparison with natural fibers, 35, 48, 57, 76–77
        (chart)
    ecological hazards, 207
    feel of, 150
    production of, 206, 207
Synthetics, 47–57, 191
    environmental, impact of, 26
    production, 26, 38–39

Tailor, 190
Taurus, 127
Tebenna, 114. *See also* Mantle
Technology, 206, 209
Temperature, 104–105
Teratogens, 35
Testes, 83
TFPI (Textile Products Identification Act), 182
Texture, 116–120
The I Can't Believe It's A Girdle, Girdle, 203
The Unfashionable Human Body, 202
Thermostatic control, 113
THPC (tetrakis hydroxy-methyl phosponium chloride),
        41. *See also* Flame retardants
THI (Temperature and Humidity Index), 197
Ties, unnecessary discomfort and, 153
Tints, 123
Tissue anoxia, 93
TLVs (Threshold Limit Values), 36
Todd, Mabel, 86
Togas, 188
Touch, 140
Toxic fumes, 146
Toxicity
    of dyes, 85
    of phenol, 180
TPO (Time, Place, and Occasion), 191
Trevira. *See* Polyesters
Triacetate fibers, 42
TRIS-BP, 40–41, 146
Trousers, choosing proper sizes of, 198
T-shirts
    kids, 150
    for women, 161

Tunic, 130
Turks, 129
Tweed, 119

Underwear, 149. *See also* Bloomers; Control Top Panties
    for cold climates, 106
    long, lined, 154
    and sexual allure, 204
Union Carbide, 53
Unisex dressing, 30, 31
Uranus, 127
Urethra. *See* Genitourinary system
Urine. *See* Genitourinary system
USASI (United States American Standards Institute), 183
Varicose veins, 82
    and poorly fitted shoes, 93
Vat dyes, 44
Vectra. *See* Olefins
Velour, 117, 150
Velvet, 117, 150
Vagina. *See* Genitourinary system
Vaginitis, 84
Value (color) 123, 124
Vasoconstriction and pain, 105
Ventral canal. *See* Skeletal system
Venus, 127
Vests, down-filled, 154
Vicuña, 72, 74
Vinyl chloride, 37
    in Saran, 56
Virgo, 127
Voluntary Industry Standards, 183
Voyeurism, 203
Waistbands, non-binding, 153
Wales, 119
Warmth
    and children's development, 143, 149
    and dress-up clothes (kids), 150
Washing. *See* Labels
Waterproof, 154
Wavelength, 122
Weaves, 118–120
Weaving, 118
White, as light, 123
Wilde, Oscar, 27, 30–31
Wool, 19, 22, 69–72
    care of, 71–72
    characteristics of, 70, 71–72
    coats, 154
    and labels, 182, 183
    and natural dresser's wardrobe, 159
    production of, 58, 70
    recommended for children, 143
    texture, 118
    types of, 182, 183
    underwear, 154
Wool Products Labeling Act, 182
Worsted, 119
Woven fabrics, 118–119
Wrap-around skirts, 133, 150, 161, 190
Wrap dresses, 161

Zefran, 52
Zippers, not to be used for kids, 149
Zodiacal cycles. *See* Planetary cycles
Zone of vasomotor control, 104

About the Authors

Maggie and Stephen Nussdorf are New York-based artists and writers. Maggie has a masters degree from the Graduate Faculty of the New School for Social Research. Her paintings and tapestries have been exhibited both here and abroad. She is a student of yoga, shiatsu, and the martial arts.

Stephen Nussdorf's study of art and architecture at the University of Michigan at Ann Arbor, the School of Visual Arts, and the Arts Student League in New York has lead him to an intensive exploration of the antiquities and, particularly, of drapery and form, a background which helped him to formulate the theory behind natural dressing. His award-winning paintings depict his fascination with the architecture of the body. He, too, is a student of yoga and shiatsu.

Maggie is a member of the Board of Governors of Artists-Craftsmen of New York. She authored the narration for the documentary film "Baba Who?"